She Delights

BIBLE STUDY

TYNDALE
MOMENTUM
A Tyndale nonfiction imprint

ELLE CARDEL

She Delights

BIBLE STUDY

A FIVE-WEEK JOURNEY TO FINDING JOY IN CHRIST

Visit Tyndale online at tyndale.com.

Visit the author online at daughterofdelight.com.

Tyndale, Tyndale's quill logo, *Tyndale Momentum*, and the Tyndale Momentum logo are registered trademarks of Tyndale House Ministries. Tyndale Momentum is a nonfiction imprint of Tyndale House Publishers, Carol Stream, Illinois.

She Delights Bible Study: A Five-Week Journey to Finding Joy in Christ

Cover designed by Jen Phelps

For information about special discounts for bulk purchases, please contact Tyndale House Publishers at csresponse@tyndale.com, or call 1-800-323-9400.

ISBN 978-1-4964-8247-1

Printed in China

31 30 29 28 27 26 25
7 6 5 4 3 2 1

To my dear sister in Christ preparing to journey her way through this study: may you meet the Lord on these pages and walk away with a heart full of devotion and utmost delight in Him and His glorious ways.

Contents

Introduction

HI, FRIEND! I'm Elle Cardel (yep, it rhymes), a sinner saved by God's glorious grace, wife to my college sweetheart, Michael, and mom to our sweet little loves, Selah and Aidan. I am also the founder of the online women's ministry Daughter of Delight, which supplies women with daily, Bible-based devotionals and gospel-centered resources to aid them in their faith walk. (Be sure to check out the *Daughter of Delight* podcast!) This study was born from my passion for teaching women Bible literacy. Needless to say, I am so glad you are here.

She Delights Bible Study can be done on its own, but I also wrote a companion book called *She Delights* that will make this experience even sweeter when you read that book alongside this study. I also recommend having your Bible, some pens, and a journal on hand. This is going to be an interactive experience and one that I pray is very rewarding and fruitful for you!

This is a five-week study. Every week, we will begin with a video teaching. Each week will include five days of study, with a two-day break before the next one begins. Video sessions can be found at TyndaleChristianResources.com. Whether you choose to go through this study individually or with a group, here are some tips to get the most out of it:

- Spend time in prayer before and after each session.
- Do what you can to remove distractions so you can remain focused during your time in this study.
- Be willing to be challenged.
- Have some of your favorite snacks on hand!
- If you are doing this study as a group, select someone to help facilitate conversation and keep you focused each time you gather.

Before you get started, know this: this study and its participants have been covered in so much prayer. We serve a God who makes no mistakes, and I believe it was His intention for you to hold this book in your hands.

It is no secret we live in a world that proudly feasts upon the lie that we can find the fulfillment our souls long for—if we delight in the pleasures of the flesh. A world that tells us the joy and satisfaction we desire in this life can be something mustered from within.

But as a people set apart in Christ, we know this could not be any further from the truth.

The world says we've got things backward and upside down, and you know what? It's right.

But in Christ, having things upside down is a good thing. A set-apart thing. Serving the unshakable, upside-down Kingdom of our righteous and holy God is why we are here.

The irony of Jesus conquering the spiritual forces of evil in order to establish His Kingdom is this: it was the ones He died for who nailed Him to the cross. In Christ, to be a leader means to be a servant. In His Kingdom, the first shall be last, suffering leads to glory, we love our enemies, and we forgive those who offend us—not just once, but seventy times seven times.

Walking in the light of Christ is completely countercultural. It will never make sense in the eyes of the world.

As we seek to be women who live in the world but are not of it, it is vital that we place our delight in the hands and heart of the One who deserves it. The One who took the death we deserve so we could be reconciled to the Father and dwell eternally with Him.

If we are not consistently immersing ourselves in the truths of God's Word and actively practicing the disciplines of delight that we find within it, we will soon find ourselves delighting in the things of this world.

My prayer for this study is that God would increase your desire to know Him and make His name known. That you would grow in your desire for and understanding of the importance of feasting on sound doctrine, imitating Christ, hating what is evil, spreading the gospel, and walking in a manner that is worthy of the holy calling you have received.

This study is not a call to perfection. It is a grace-filled invitation to seek first the Kingdom of God in all of life. It is an invitation to participate in the things that are holy and right and good in the eyes of the Lord: the things that will increase your delight in and love for Him and that God will use to fashion you into the likeness of Christ.

Thank you for entrusting me with your time and for the opportunity to lead you. May the Lord use *She Delights Bible Study* to bless you, challenge you, and grow you in your delight of His glorious ways. May God use our time together to convict us and increase our joy in being His daughters of delight.

Soli Deo Gloria!

SESSION 1 VIEWER GUIDE

Pursue Sound Doctrine

Recommended Reading: Chapters 1 and 2 of *She Delights*

notes

PREPARING FOR THE SESSION: As you prepare to get started, reflect on and/or discuss the following questions:

- What role does God's Word play in your life right now?
- How would you define "sound doctrine"?
- What struggles or questions do you have when it comes to Bible study?

DURING THE SESSION: Use the space above to jot down notes from Elle's teaching.

TAKEAWAY TIME: What stood out to you most about this session?

PRAY: End your time in prayer, thanking God for the powerful, life-changing gift that is His Word!

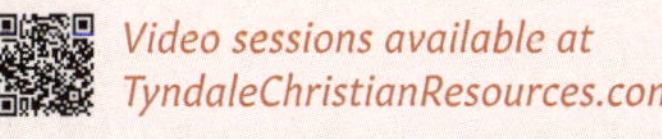
Video sessions available at TyndaleChristianResources.com

Why Sound Doctrine?

"IF YOU'RE PRAYING FOR IT, IT'S GOING TO HAPPEN."

I was sitting in a coffee shop working on the proposal for my first book when I heard these very words spoken from across the room.

I looked up to see two brothers in Christ sitting in the corner, one encouraging the other with this well-intentioned but spiritually toxic statement.

Now, I'm not one to intentionally intrude on the conversations of others. I may be from the South, but I really *was* minding my own business! For some reason, though, the Lord often uses coffee shops to open my eyes to the need for greater biblical literacy among Christians. The irony here is, I'm often working on biblical literacy resources (like this study, for example) while I'm in these coffee shops. Perhaps it's God's way of keeping my flame lit for teaching women how to study the Bible.

In full transparency, there was a lengthy season of my life when I would not have seen anything wrong with the statement I overheard. A time where I would have found a tremendous amount of comfort and encouragement in those words.

I am so thankful this is no longer the case.

This statement is simply not biblically accurate. Perhaps this man was referring to James 4:2, which says, "You do not have, because you do not ask." If we read this as a stand-alone verse, it is easy to see how we could think it means that God will give us what we want as long as we ask for it. However, reading the verse in context reveals that this is not at all what James is getting at. If you read James 4:1-3, you will see that the people James addressed here were covetous, to the point where they were willing to fight—even kill—in order to get what they wanted. Any prayers from the lips of these people were spoken from a place of selfish gain.

Here's the thing: just because we eagerly pray for something does not guarantee God is going to give it to us. This is because God does not delight in our selfish desires; He delights in giving us what He knows we truly need (see Psalm 145:9; Philippians 4:19). Just because something we pray for seems good to us does not mean it *is* good for us. Nor does God invite us to participate in a reward system that determines what He does and does not do for us.

Everything God does—*absolutely, positively everything*—derives from His perfect and sovereign will. This is nothing short of good news for us!

The reality of being human is that our desires do not always align with God's desires. This is the case for me more often than not. Our emotions are fickle things, and if we are honest with ourselves, it can be easier to base the decisions we make on how we are feeling rather than on God's Word.

Thankfully, we do not serve a God who does what He wants based on how He wakes up feeling each day. Unlike our emotions, God never changes. This should offer us a tremendous amount of comfort!

But I get it.

I know how challenging it can be to trust in the Lord over our emotions. Our emotions are not inherently bad. After all, God gave them to us, and He makes no mistakes. Emotions are a very real part of being human. Although they do not belong on the throne of our hearts like our great God does, there is a purpose and place for them. We just have to make sure we don't place them above the Lord.

The more we plant ourselves in the Word, the easier this becomes.

When we are not actively saturating our hearts in Scripture, our desire to live in alignment with God's will begins to fade and, once again, our gaze turns back on ourselves.

But when we choose to fill our hearts with the truths of God's Word, the opposite begins to take place. We start to understand what it means to truly delight in the Lord. We begin to embrace and rejoice in the truth that God only has His best in mind for us, even when it may not appear that way. We find ourselves believing the words of 1 John 5:14-15, which says if we pray with confidence—"if we ask anything according to his will"—"he hears us," and "we have the requests that we have asked of him." This means praying "Thy will be done" from a place of utmost surrender and trust in the Father's heart.

No matter how a situation turns out, our desire for God's will should always take precedence over the temptation to do things our way. For only the One who first breathed life into us—the One who first loved us—knows what is best for His own. And thanks be to God for that, amen?

God has revealed exactly what He wants us to know through His holy, infallible Word. He gave us His Word to be a lamp to our feet and a light to our path (see Psalm 119:105).

Statements like "If you're praying for it, it's going to happen" draw us away from the heart of who God is, not closer.

The best way to be on guard against what sounds good about God but is not true—also known as a sugarcoated gospel—is to take on the responsibility of knowing what Scripture says.

I have said it before and I will say it again and again: in order to know God, we must know His Word.

Biblical illiteracy is not the answer. It simply does not sustain. When I get out of the habit of reading my Bible, nothing good comes from it. I become distracted with myself rather than attentive to the only One who deserves my focus. I become spiritually malnourished. Rather than being guided by the truths of God's Word, I am guided by my fleeting emotions.

My sister, when we know the Word, we will know the truth God desires for us to live by.

When we know the Word, we will be able to discern whether something that feels and sounds good truly lines up with sound doctrine.

When we know the Word, we will be more equipped to remain steadfast in our fight against the ways of this world.

When we know the Word, we will become more like Christ. For the truth sets us free and changes us from the inside out.

Get to know the God of the Holy Scriptures. Delight in walking in obedience and sharing the Good News of the glorious gospel of our Lord Jesus Christ!

Take a moment to reflect on where you are at in your Bible literacy journey, in addition to any goals you have for your time in this study.

DAY 1:

It Starts with Us

YOU ARE A THEOLOGIAN.

Do you agree or disagree with this statement? Why?

Years ago, when I was a college student studying theology, if you would have asked me if I agreed with the above statement, I would have said no.

Me? A theologian? No way!

Often when we hear words like *theologian* or *theology*, our minds immediately jump to Dietrich Bonhoeffer, C. S. Lewis, R. C. Sproul, John Piper . . . the list goes on. But as wonderful as it is to glean from their wisdom, not everyone is a scholar.

Did you catch that? You do not have to be a scholar to be a theologian.

The word *theology* comes from combining two Greek words: *theos*, which means "God," and *logos*, which means "word" or "reasoning." When you put the two together, you have *theology*, our thoughts and understanding concerning God.

Here is what this means for us: any effort we put in to understand the Bible—spending time in the Word, sitting under the teachings of our pastor, engaging in conversation centered on God—literally anything we do to explore the truths of Scripture contributes to our theological understanding.

Therefore, you, my friend, are a theologian.

The most important question that immediately follows this realization should be "Is my theology rooted in sound doctrine?"

You Are a Theologian

When you hear the word *doctrine*, what comes to mind?

Before you start to feel overwhelmed by this word or roll your eyes at its dry lack of appeal, please let me explain why I believe it is so important—vital, even—for us to engage in the depths of doctrine.

Many people believe they can know God outside of Scripture. I believe we can experience God outside of His Word but knowing Him first starts within it. Too often, we take the wrongful approach of placing the responsibility to know what God's Word says in the hands of our preachers and Bible teachers, but this is not a healthy perspective to have. In fact, it places in the hands of people what only God can do in us through His Word, and this is incredibly dangerous. While there *is* a very necessary and vital role that the church plays in the Christian walk, knowing God's Word first starts with us and our Holy Father. To believe otherwise implies a belief that the Bible is not infallible. It encourages the believer to try to know Christ based on what they have been told by others, how they feel about Him, or how they think He operates rather than understanding who He is through the authoritative lens of Scripture. How are we to learn anything about Jesus at all if we are not immersed in the depth, beauty, and truth of God's Word? If we care about Jesus, we should also care about doctrine and theology. As Jesus says in Matthew 4:4, "People do not live by bread alone, but by every word that comes from the mouth of God" (NLT).

In Matthew 22:37-38, Jesus says, "'You must love the LORD your God with all your heart, all your soul, and all your mind.' This is the first and greatest commandment" (NLT).

In order to genuinely love and authentically worship God, we must know who He is. We cannot love someone without first knowing them. We cannot be changed by truth if we do not know it. A quote I once stumbled upon by A. W. Tozer says, "What comes into our minds when we think about God is the most important thing about us."[1]

What comes to mind when you think about God? Take some time to reflect on this question and write out your thoughts below. Be honest with yourself. It's just you and the Lord here. (And He already knows and loves you, no matter what!)

The Impact of Our Theology

So how do we love the Lord our God with all of our heart, soul, and mind? How do we obey the first and greatest commandment?

By picking up our Bibles and planting ourselves in them. By concerning ourselves with biblical theology—the study of the doctrines found in Scripture—and delighting in the opportunity to know God in the ways He reveals Himself to us through His Word. By caring enough to know what we believe and why we believe it as a result of our time in the Word.

In Matthew 22:39, Jesus continues with, "A second is equally important: 'Love your neighbor as yourself'" (NLT).

Do you know what this means?

Our theology not only influences our understanding and worship of God but the way we love others as well! The more we seek to understand God's character and be fashioned in His likeness, the better we can love others as God loves us.

My sister, biblical theology is a prerequisite for godly living. It impacts *every* facet of life:

- How we worship.
- How we speak.
- How much time we spend in the Bible.
- How we respond to a needy friend when we are exhausted.
- How we mother our children and tend to our home.

- How we invest in the church.
- What we prioritize.
- How we express our emotions.
- How we pour into others.
- How we steward our finances.
- How we view ourselves.

The list is endless, isn't it?

What else would you add to this list?

As our love for theology grows and permeates the things we do, let us not forget this:

The call to be theologians is not for the sake of debating divisive subjects or priding ourselves on knowing everything about the Bible. (Note: theology does not hold all the answers to our questions.) It is for the sake of knowing, embodying, and glorifying Christ in all of life. It is for the sake of love. As Paul says in 1 Corinthians 8:1, "While knowledge makes us feel important, it is love that strengthens the church" (NLT).

Read 2 Timothy 3:16 and take heart in its truths as you fill in the blanks below:

All Scripture is ____________ by God and is useful to ____________ us what is ____________ and to make us realize what is ____________ in our lives. It ____________ us when we are ____________ and ____________ us to do what is ____________. (NLT)

All of Scripture—not just some of it—is God-breathed, God-inspired, and alive. It was written for God's glory, our good, and the good of others!

May we be women of God who love Him enough to delight in knowing Him through His Word, who embrace and embody a sound theology that is rooted in truth and love for all the world to see.

Jot down any thoughts, questions, or concerns you have related to biblical theology.

Write down how you would respond to someone if they asked you, "Why is biblical theology important?"

Is there anything holding you back from diving into the depths of God's Word?

Get excited! Tomorrow we are going to begin exploring the necessary steps for pursuing sound biblical theology. I cannot wait to dive into all the goodness with you!

DAY 2:
How Not to Read Your Bible

I AM CONVINCED THAT SATAN is on a mission to make us believe the Bible is centered on us.

But this could not be any further from the truth.

There is a wrong way to read the Bible, and it is done when we make ourselves the focus of God's Word instead of God Himself. When we do this, the intent of Scripture gets obscured, and our view of God is diminished. We glorify ourselves over the One who deserves all the glory, honor, and praise.

My friend, the Bible is not a self-help book. From its first page to its last, every word of Scripture is about God.

Who He is.

How He operates.

What He longs for us to know about Him.

All these things are found in the gift of His Word to His people.

The truths of Scripture do not always feel good to read. They will often offend the flesh. But as we lean in to seeking God through Scripture in the ways that He intends, my prayer for both you and me is that we would allow the things that don't feel good to humble us and leave us in awe of who He is. For He is perfect in all His attributes and all His ways.

I'm not saying the Bible does not speak to who we are and reveal the path we are called to walk. It does indeed do this! But if we open our Bibles and first look for *ourselves* instead of searching for our Father, we misunderstand the purpose and gift of God's Word. If we first ask "What does this mean for me?" instead of "God, what does this passage reveal about who You are?" we will certainly risk misinterpreting the text.

Take the story of David and Goliath, for example. If we read this story with only the question of "What does this mean for me?" (see the eisegesis section below), we instantly place ourselves in David's shoes and view Goliath as the trial in life we are currently facing. If we sling our stones—which represent our faith in this case—we are able to overcome said trial. That doesn't sound so bad, does it? What it is actually doing, however, is making ourselves rather than God the savior of the story and encouraging us to continue reading biblical narratives in this way.

If we read the story of David and Goliath correctly (see the exegesis section below), meaning we approach Scripture with the question of "What is God revealing about Himself here?," the outcome is much different. By exploring the historical and literary context of this passage, we learn that many of the events of David's life foreshadowed the life of Jesus. The story of David and Goliath points to the reality that Jesus is the only one who can prevail against the dominion of darkness and the power of Satan.

Scripture tells us who we are in light of who God is. Knowing God enables us to know ourselves, to recognize how perfect and selfless He is and how depraved and sinful we are.

If our time in the Word is not reflective of this truth, if it does not lead us to behold God's glory, we are missing the mark. We are being pushed further and further away from the story God has put on full display in Scripture: His plan to rescue His people from sin through the life, death, and resurrection of His Son, Jesus Christ.

The purpose of reading the stories that fill the pages of Scripture is not just learning from the ordinary people found in them or putting ourselves in their shoes, but rather encountering the One to whom their stories point and reveal—the central character of the Bible and the One our lives should be centered around: Jesus Christ, the Savior of the world. I like to think of it this way: the Old Testament points to Jesus, whereas the New Testament reveals Jesus. For example, Isaiah 53:3 prophesies, "He was despised and rejected—a man of sorrows, acquainted with deepest grief. We turned our backs on him and looked the other way. He was despised, and we did not care" (NLT). The fulfillment of this prophecy is found through the person of Christ, as revealed in John 1:10-11: "He came into the very world he created, but the world didn't recognize him. He came to his own people, and even they rejected him" (NLT). *Everything* is connected to Jesus!

I don't know about you, but I want to read God's Word in a way that asks *How does this point me to my need for Christ?* in such a way that it humbles me and draws me closer to Him and away from myself.

The gospel changes *everything*. May the power of God at work in us and our time spent in His Word be reflective of this truth.

Identifying Eisegesis

Read John 5:16-18 and 5:39-40. Describe what happens.

The Jewish leaders we read of here approached Scripture believing it offered them eternal life apart from Jesus. *Yikes!* This is why Jesus very clearly tells them that all of Scripture points to Him—because they were reading it for their own selfish gain. One commentator puts it like this: "They read it not to search for God but to find arguments to support their own positions. They did not really love God; they loved their own ideas about him."[1]

Describe a time when you misused Scripture to justify how you felt about something, or a time when you witnessed someone else do this. What did you learn from the experience?

The word *eisegesis* describes what the Jewish leaders were doing, and what many Christians today continue to do. Eisegesis refers to the practice of inserting one's own ideas into Scripture. The tendency with eisegesis is to interpret Scripture in a way that reflects one's own bias and beliefs rather than what it actually means. When we eisegete Scripture, we force it to give us what we want, to say things it does not really say.

In order to know who we are, we must first know who God is. Let us not miss the mark on this. Eternal life is not found in reading Scriptures with our own bias, like the Jewish leaders believed. It is found through the One whom the Scriptures proclaim! It is found in knowing and beholding our eternal, everlasting, unchanging, and almighty God. The Bible is how God reveals Himself to us. Everything else unfolds from this understanding.

Exploring Exegesis

As we work to refrain from eisegesis, let us focus our efforts on exegesis. Whereas eisegesis gives us what we want, exegesis gives us what we need—and what our Father in heaven wants us to have—the powerful, authoritative truths of His Word.

Read Hebrews 4:12 and 2 Timothy 3:16. Based on these verses, why is Bible study important?

What challenges do you currently face in your Bible study? Why do you struggle in those areas?

What excites you most about reading and studying God's Word?

In Christ, we have the wisdom and influence of God's Word and the power of His Holy Spirit in us! We are complete in Him alone. Hallelujah!

That said, our flesh will attempt to tell us otherwise. We must live aware of our nature to seek what is wrong and fleeting. We must always be on guard. A sugar-coated gospel may make us feel good, but it has severe long-term effects. It robs us of greater opportunities to connect with Christ. It robs us of truly knowing God.

May this not be the case for us. May we be women who delight in theology, the pursuit of knowledge and wisdom in Christ!

For the rest of our time together this week, we will explore how to properly read, study, and apply the truths of God's Word to all of life. I am both eager and excited to walk through this together. And get excited because tomorrow is just the beginning!

DAY 3:
Questioning Scripture

WELCOME TO DAY THREE of laying the foundation for a joyful pursuit of sound doctrine! So far, we have explored the need for and importance of this life-changing gift, in addition to what God says about His Word. Our theology—our understanding of who God is, how He works, and who we are in light of who He is and what He has done for us—impacts *everything* we do.

The beautiful gift of sound doctrine offers us so much:

- It encourages and edifies.
- It fashions us in Christ's likeness.
- It instills the glorious hope of our Lord Jesus Christ.
- It offers us a direct line of communication to God the Father!

Over the course of the next three days, we are going to explore some tried-and-true steps for studying and applying God's Word to all of life.

The steps I will share with you are both simple and necessary. Although they are straightforward, they require intentionality and effort. This is where things can start to get a little (or a lot) tricky.

There is no overnight quick fix when it comes to opening our Bibles as much as we would like to. Like anything else, this is a discipline. We must be patient and gracious with ourselves every step of the way and look to the Lord for the strength to remain steadfast.

As we work toward building and implementing the spiritual discipline of intimately knowing our Father in heaven through His Word, I want to encourage you to focus not on your motivation (or lack thereof) as the source of fuel for the journey, but on God's grace and glory.

If you are struggling to get into the Word because the desire to do so is just not there, please hear me when I say you are not alone. This is a very real example of the war raging between our flesh and spirit. There will be days we give in and choose not to pick up our Bible. When this happens, take heart, for God's grace abounds. Praise Him!

Just as the opportunity to know God is a gift, the opportunity to try again when we fail is too.

Be fueled by the Father's grace and glory and how He continues to reveal Himself to you, my sister. His strength is made perfect in our every weakness.

Spend some time writing down the truth-filled words of 2 Corinthians 12:9 on repeat until they feel like a breath of fresh air and a balm to your soul.

Yield your heart to God's and ask that His strength would be made your own as you pick up your Bible and prepare to dive in.

You will have no regrets in doing so. This I promise you. Your Father in heaven awaits your presence!

Embracing Our Questions

I can remember having questions about Scripture and feeling embarrassed.

Even when I was a child, Satan was at war with my mind, trying to convince me that I should know better; that my questions would make me look like I didn't really know my Bible. Insecurity almost always took over and kept me quiet, as my list of questions continued to silently grow over time.

Whether we show up to the Word unprepared or armed and ready to give our best attempt at undistracted time in His presence, the questions will come.

When they do, know this: God delights in the ways you are searching to know and understand Him. Your questions are a reflection of this truth. Satan wants you to focus on fear and shame—anything that will lead you away from time spent in the Word—but the Lord wants you to feel free to ask whatever it is that comes to mind. He knows your heart, my sister. He wants you near.

The beauty of asking questions and putting time and effort into understanding them through the lens of Scripture is that growth and maturation will follow. The more time we spend in God's Word, the more we will grow in our knowledge of God and the things He desires for us to know—and the more we will be shaped and strengthened by His Word. Our efforts will surely be blessed!

Does this mean Scripture will answer all of our questions? Certainly not. God does not promise us that the answer to every question is found within His Word. Is that a mistake on His part? Certainly not. God has revealed in the Bible exactly what He wants us to know. The truth is, you will likely have unanswered questions for the rest of your days on this side of heaven. (Hey, welcome to the club!)

But one day, when we're face-to-face with Jesus, it will *all make sense*. We may not be able to see the bigger picture right now, but one day we will receive the understanding our souls crave. Peace and joy will flood our hearts in ways that we have not yet known. What a wonderful day this will be!

Take a moment to write down, *shame-free,* any questions concerning Scripture or the character of God you desire to explore.

Keep seeking and asking, my sister. Keep drawing near. The Lord will meet you and bless your efforts.

Speaking of questions, let's take a look at some helpful and important questions to ask as we spend time studying the Word. These questions will offer both clarity and confidence, and perhaps bring even more questions to the surface in our journey toward understanding Scripture.

The Ask Phase

I recommend asking three types of questions whenever you read Scripture. They are:

1. What is the historical context?
2. What is the literary context?
3. What additional questions do I have about the text?

Context is key when it comes to our Bible study! Say it with me: *Context is key!* Knowing the who, what, when, where, and why of Scripture helps us to understand the original setting it was written in and the original audience it was written to. Knowing the context of Scripture helps us to avoid misinterpreting and misusing it. It paves the way for the Bible to speak for itself. It is only when we understand the originality of a passage that we can faithfully apply its takeaways to the modern day.

The Historical Context

Did you enjoy history growing up? I found it interesting at times but mostly boring, if I am being honest. However, now that I am older, and especially where Scripture is concerned, I get excited about it.

One of the best ways to gain an understanding of the timeless truths of Scripture is to explore the historicity behind it. Each book of the Bible was written at a specific time. Familiarizing ourselves with the historical background is necessary as we journey through Scripture.

The historical context refers to the time a passage was written, who it was written by, who it was written for, where it was written, and what the culture was like during this time period.

Putting in the work to understand the context can feel tedious at times, but it is so rewarding! When we do this, we notice things we would otherwise miss out on.

We learn to see the passage in the ways its intended audience would have received it. And I don't know about you, but I want to know as much about Scripture as there is to know!

Take Revelation 3:17, for example. Referring to the city of Laodicea, Jesus calls them "blind and naked." Laodicea was a city known for its fine linens and eye salves. This city was prospering, and its residents had a high view of themselves. Jesus struck at the heart of their pride, saying that although they might have the clearest vision and be the best dressed physically, spiritually they were the most blind and naked people He knew. They were in need of what only He could offer them.

It would be impossible to make this connection without first learning about Laodicea during the time Revelation was written.

No matter what part of Scripture we study, we can discover implications like these when we seek the historical context.

When we come to a historical passage, it's helpful to ask the five Ws: who, what, when, where, and why.

- Who wrote this?
- What was the culture/political climate like during this time?
- When was this written?
- Where was this written?
- Why did the author write this?

Perhaps you are thinking, *These are fine questions and all, Elle, but how do I find the answers to them?*

Ah, I'm so very glad you asked, my friend!

Answering these questions without the proper resources can feel *very* overwhelming and nearly impossible (and understandably so). Here are some resources I recommend having on hand as you immerse yourself in the historical context pertaining to a specific passage of Scripture.

- study Bible
- Bible dictionary

- Bible encyclopedia
- commentaries

If you can only invest in one of these things, I highly recommend researching and purchasing a good study Bible. Fun fact: you can likely access the remaining resources through your local library, and you can also access many of them online for free.

Once I have my resources ready to go, I refer to the book introduction in my study Bible to gain a baseline understanding of the historical context of the book I am about to read.

Let me add—*and it is important I say this*—I only utilize resources like commentaries, study Bible notes, etc., after I have first prioritized hearing God's voice. That means I first spend time in Scripture and prayer. I admit my need for help and ask the Spirit to reveal the wisdom and truth the Lord has in store for me as I read His Word. During this time, I make note of any words, phrases, places, questions, or connections I make along the way. Commentaries, study Bibles, and all other biblical resources are great things to have on hand, but they remain closed during this time. This is because I never want to prioritize the voice of man—no matter how scholarly, easy-to-read, wise, and helpful it may sound—over the voice of God.

The Father's faithful, unchanging voice comes first. *Always.*

The Literary Context

Next, let's dive into the literary context. The Bible is filled with a variety of literary styles and utilizes many literary techniques, including figurative language, imagery, allusions, and foreshadowing. To ensure a thorough understanding of a passage, it is very important to familiarize yourself with biblical genres and literary devices. The primary categories of biblical genres are narrative, law, poetry, wisdom, prophecy, gospel, letter, and history. When we understand the genre in which the passage we are studying was written, we are able to more accurately interpret and apply it.

Knowing the literary context also offers us the support needed to refrain from participating in the dangers of eisegesis. (Please refer back to day two for more on this subject.)

God made no mistakes in organizing Scripture the way He has. It is not meant to be read one random passage at a time, but in a more methodical way. Here's why: from start to finish, the Bible tells one cohesive story made up of history books, letters, songs, and poetry—all composing a complete work centered on who Jesus is and what He has done. There is meaning in every word of every verse on every page. It all works together, in unity, to tell the story of redemption from beginning to end. Let us do our best to read and study God's Word in ways that put this beautiful truth on display.

THE MOST IMPORTANT QUESTION

"What is the point?" is the most important contextual question to ask when looking at Scripture.

To get a solid grasp of the literary context, it is important that we understand the genre of the book of the Bible we're reading and read the passage within its entire context.

Here is what I mean: Do not just read the passage you desire to better understand. I encourage you to read the entire book if possible. If it's a lengthy book or you don't have time, read the chapter that the passage is in, along with the chapter before and the chapter after it. This will help you understand the setting, themes, and broader idea of the passage as well.

When we place value on literary context, it becomes harder to make God's Word about us. And that's a good thing, wouldn't you agree?

Literary context is the key to understanding the role your passage of study plays in the story of Scripture. It will also help open your eyes to why it is placed where it is within God's Word.

THE LOVE CHAPTER

Let's explore the need for grasping literary context through the "love chapter." If you have been to a wedding or if you are married, you likely know exactly what chapter I am referring to: 1 Corinthians 13.

If you have a study Bible, grab it and open up to this chapter. If you do not, you can access an introduction to 1 Corinthians on the website Blue Letter Bible (blueletterbible.org), a resource I personally love and recommend.

Spend some time familiarizing yourself with the historical background of this letter. Note your observations below.

Once you have a good grip on the historical background of 1 Corinthians, it's time to saturate yourself in it. Take your time reading through this letter. (It is okay if you have to do this in more than one sitting, but this step is important.) Write down any themes you spot, observations you note, and questions you have along the way.

Now that you have read 1 Corinthians all the way through, read chapters 12–14. Continue to make note of anything that stands out to you (words, phrases, places) and additional questions.

Finally, plant yourself in 1 Corinthians 13. How do you feel when you read this chapter? Why?

It is likely 1 Corinthians 13 makes you feel hopeful, warm, comfortable, and secure. But did you know that this chapter was not intended to be read at weddings or featured on a Valentine's Day or anniversary card? It is easy to misunderstand Paul's intent if we neglect the context surrounding this passage.

If you read the chapters that sandwich 1 Corinthians 13, you will discover that the Corinthian church was becoming divided over matters related to spiritual gifts. Paul wrote this letter to them not to take a side but to make the point that they should pursue love despite their differences.

Paul is not writing about how love *feels*. He is conveying what it looks like when it's lived out. His point is that true love is demonstrated by actions, not mere words. In fact, the Greek word for "love" he uses here, *agape*, refers to love that is rooted in "self-denial for the sake of another."[1]

Although we use this passage at wedding ceremonies, its true contextual purpose is to encourage reconciliation in the church fueled by love in action.

Additional Questions

As alluded to earlier, it is impossible to study Scripture without having questions. But do not shy away from them. Embrace them by laying them at the Father's feet as you seek His understanding. Here is a list of questions that may be helpful to refer to as you study. Be sure to add your own as they come to mind!

- What is going on in the passage?
- Who are the main characters?
- Whom can I identify with and why?
- What is the sequence of events?
- What is the main conflict of the text? What caused it?
- What type of change does this text demand of me?
- How can I see God's sovereign hand at work in this passage?
- Are there any prophecies or parallels to Christ?
- Are there any connections to this text elsewhere in the Bible?
- What are the takeaways of the text for the audience, then and now?

Piecing It All Together

Ready to complete the Ask phase of the Bible study process? I've got a challenge for you! Turn in your Bible to James 1:22-25 and practice implementing the Ask phase in the space below. (See page 20 for a reminder of what this phase looks like.)

Great job, friend! I hope you are starting to feel equipped, encouraged, and excited to take what you learn and dig deep.

Tomorrow we will explore the second and third phases of the Bible study process: analyzing Scripture and applying what we learn to everyday life.

Until then!

DAY 4:

Analyzing and Applying Scripture

IF YOU KNOW ME, you know I love to read and write.

My love for reading was a result of being introduced to the Nancy Drew books as a child. I could not put them down, and truth be told, I cannot wait to read them with my daughter when she is old enough.

Writing, however, came a little later in life. I discovered my love for it during high school, but it really began to blossom during my college years.

My major (theology) was centered around writing more than anything else. I loved this because multiple-choice *anything* was my academic enemy.

While studying theology, I learned how to write lengthy papers focused on God's Word. One of my greatest academic accomplishments was the seventeen-page paper I wrote on the Lord's Supper.

My time learning how to research and write these papers fostered a love for doing more and more of it outside of the classroom.

Now here I am, getting to share these very tools with you! What a precious gift.

Today we are going to walk through the Analyze and Apply phases to connect the truths of Scripture to everyday life.

Are you as excited as I am? Maybe not, and that's okay! Either way, the goal is to feel more confident approaching Scripture, which is what matters most. So let's get to it, shall we?

Analyzing Scripture

First, let's talk about analyzing. This phase comes *after* we have spent time seeking and listening to God through Scripture. It also comes after we have noted any questions or things that stuck out to us when we read and reflected on the passage.

This step consists of exploring third-party resources to help us answer questions and consider the context and meaning of Scripture. These resources include commentaries, study Bibles, Bible encyclopedias, Bible dictionaries, and any additional materials (sermons, articles, podcasts, books, etc.) that you might find helpful in coming to a deeper understanding of your selected passage.

Today, I want to take an in-depth look at Matthew 18:20: "Where two or three are gathered in my name, there am I among them." Go ahead and grab your Bible, study Bible, and computer or phone.

The book of Matthew is a firsthand account of Jesus' life, ministry, death, and resurrection. It comes to us some 400 years after the end of the Old Testament. Throughout it, Jesus teaches people what it looks like to be part of His Kingdom, "the Kingdom of Heaven."

As we prepare to study Matthew 18:20, let's spend some time familiarizing ourselves with this Gospel and its author. To do so, go to blueletterbible.org on your computer or phone. Once you have arrived, click on "Study" at the top of the page. From there, look for the section titled "Bible Reference" and click on "Introductions to the Bible." Scroll down until you find Matthew, then click on "BLB | The Gospel of Matthew."

Spend some time reading through Blue Letter Bible's introduction to Matthew and note what you find helpful in the space below.

My Key Takeaways

- Matthew's original name was Levi (Mark 2:14). He left everything he knew in order to follow Jesus.[1]
- Only once, while listing out the twelve apostles, does Matthew refer to himself as a tax collector (10:3). His former name, Levi, is used more often than the name Matthew to reference his sinful past.[2]

- It seems as if Matthew wrote this Gospel with Jews in mind and with the goal of proving and proclaiming Jesus as the Messianic King of Old Testament prophecy. He does so by quoting passages from Old Testament prophecies more than sixty times.[3]
- The term "Kingdom of Heaven" appears thirty times in Matthew and nowhere else in the rest of Scripture.[4]

Now that we have spent time familiarizing ourselves with this Gospel, let's turn our attention to Matthew 18:20 and explore its meaning for the time he wrote it and now.

Read Matthew 18:20. What implications and/or questions arise from reading this verse on its own?

My Questions about This Passage

- Who is Jesus speaking to?
- Why did Jesus say this?
- Why would it be necessary for two or three to be gathered in prayer in order for Jesus to be present?
- Isn't Jesus already present in the life of each individual believer?
- Since Jesus refers specifically to a group of two or three, would this apply to groups larger than that?

When we read Matthew 18:20 as a stand-alone verse, it is easy to misunderstand it. Many modern-day Christians use this verse to affirm the value of small prayer meetings or church gatherings.

However, is this what Jesus is actually getting at? The simple answer is no, but let's implement the proper steps to faithfully and confidently determine this for ourselves.

Read Matthew 18:15-20 two to three times. Jot down any questions and observations you have as you do so. Once you finish, type "Matthew 18" in the search bar of blueletterbible.org and scroll until you get to Matthew 18:20. From here, click on "Tools" beside the verse. Then click "Commentaries." Spend time reading what different commentators have to say and note what you find helpful in the space below.

My Questions about This Passage

- What does Jesus mean when He says, "let him be to you as a Gentile and a tax collector" (verse 17)? Interesting how Matthew, the author of this Gospel, used to be a tax collector himself.
- In the context of church discipline, what does it mean to bind and loose (verse 18)?

My Observations about This Passage

- Jesus is talking about church discipline (confronting sin and resolving disputes to keep the church in obedience to God). He emphasizes that this responsibility should not be on the shoulders of just one person but shared by two or three.
- Here's the church discipline process, as outlined by Jesus:

STEP 1: Private confrontation. Prayerfully go to the offending brother or sister on your own first, with the motive of reconciliation.
STEP 2: Expand the circle. If the person listens, receives what you tell them, and repents, the problem has been resolved and there is reason to rejoice. If

the person continues to live in unrepentant sin, it is then time to involve a few others.

STEP 3: Bring it before the church. If the two or three involved have spoken to the unrepentant person and he or she remains unrepentant, they are to continue in prayer and make church leadership aware. This could ultimately result in the unrepentant brother or sister being removed from the gift of fellowship (the church). But those involved in this difficult decision can (and should) take heart, knowing that it is honoring to the Lord and Jesus is with them as they continue to pray that God will work in this person's heart and ultimately restore them to the church.

What differences did you notice when you read Matthew 18:20 as a stand-alone verse compared with reading and studying it as part of the whole of Matthew 18:15-20? Note your key takeaways below.

Applying Scripture

Now it is time to piece it all together. Reflect on what you have learned and take some time to answer the questions below to embrace and apply your new understanding of Matthew 18:20 to your faith walk.

According to verse 15, what is the purpose of going and telling "your brother" his sin? What are some reasons why you should first pursue private confrontation regarding another believer's sin?

Describe what loving confrontation looks like.

What is your typical reaction when someone sins against you? Do you ignore them? Retaliate? Harbor your hurt? Do you take time to prayerfully consider how to respond?

Have you ever witnessed church discipline in action? If yes, reflect on how it was carried out in light of Matthew 18:15-20. If not, jot down some reasons why the practice of church discipline may be lacking in churches today.

How can you apply what you have learned about Matthew 18:15-20 to your faith walk?

My Key Takeaways

- On its own, Matthew 18:20 can sound as if Jesus is speaking about His presence during the prayers of small-group gatherings. This might make the reader wonder whether or not He is present for the private prayers of each individual Christian and the prayers of groups larger than three people.
- When read within its proper contextual setting, this verse begins to unfold in a whole new way. It is not about having the correct number of people to pray but how to discipline an unrepentant brother or sister in Christ in a way that honors God and His vision for the church.
- Although Jesus is present in every believer's life, here He is not speaking to His presence in our prayer meetings or church gatherings. He is referring to His presence in the context of church discipline.
- Here in Matthew 18, Jesus refers to an Old Testament law (Deuteronomy 19:15) that says an accusation from one person is not enough to establish a case against someone. Two or three witnesses who are in agreement, however, are able to bring a charge. But whereas this Old Testament law is about action within a human court, the words of Jesus here in Matthew 18 refer to the "heavenly court." This is why Jesus assures us He is with the two to three who have gathered in His name: because executing discipline within the church is both necessary and right in the eyes of the Lord. As we do so, we can take heart in the truth that no matter how difficult discipline may be, Christ is with us every step of the way.
- Considering that Jesus spent a lot of His time with Gentiles and tax collectors (see Matthew 9:10-13), His call to let the unrepentant sinner "be to you as a Gentile and a tax collector" demonstrates that we should still love the person under discipline, even if they are no longer part of the church community.
- Binding and loosing: Jesus gives the local church authority to make binding decisions when it comes to church discipline. This means church leadership has the right to bind—or forbid—an unrepentant member from church fellowship. In addition, the local church has the authority to loose—or permit—a member to stay or return when they have a repentant heart.

A Message for the Church

The message of Matthew 18:15-20 is just as applicable for Christians today as it was for those Jesus first spoke these words to. Confrontation is not comfortable, which is why we tend to avoid it at all costs or put it off for as long as we can. But there is a way to go about it that honors the Lord: finding our comfort and confidence in Christ and confronting the other person out of love. When we do this, we begin to care more about the person's soul than we do our relationship with them.

Church discipline may not be easy, but God has sanctioned it as good and fruitful for the health of His church. It is hard to call out sin in others, and it hurts to have sin called out in us. But the accountability that comes from this act is meant to be fruitful and edifying.

This passage is a powerful reminder to all Christians that we were not made to do this life alone. We were made for community and at the heart of a healthy church body is accountability and discipline. As we seek to follow the guidelines for discipline in this passage, we can rest assured, for Jesus promises His presence when we are gathered in His name.

Why is it important to read the Bible in context?

Name the types of context we should explore when studying a Scripture passage.

In what ways do you find it difficult to confront others about their sin? How does Matthew 18:15-20 speak to this?

DAY 5:

Light in the Darkness

I DO NOT LIKE THE DARK, but I am not a big artificial light person, either. Natural light, however? I'll take it *all*, please! If I need extra light, I either pull the curtains back or fill the room with warm light offered by the lamps I have all over the house.

My favorite type of light is offered once a day at dusk, or golden hour. There is something special about this window of time that makes me pause to savor the beauty of the setting sun. The golden hues of its rays paired with the warm palette of the evening sky often takes my breath away.

This lovely time of day brings me a warm and welcome peace that points me to the greatest Light of all: my Lord and Savior, Jesus Christ.

As we make our way through the final day of our week focused on pursuing sound doctrine, we do so with a special focus on the light of life—that is, the light of Christ. When we follow Jesus, we become daughters of light. Jesus' light leads and illuminates. It helps us to see and understand things we couldn't otherwise. It enables us to recognize our sin and helps us put it to death. It allows us to understand the message of the gospel and bear witness to it. There is no other light but His, and it will never go out.

Read and record below the words of John 8:12.

When you picture the light of life, what do you see?

Through Jesus, the light of God's presence shines. This light is the purest light there is and will ever be.

Read 1 John 1:5. What does it reveal about God's light?

How blessed are we to belong to a God who is pure and perfect in all He does, who cannot be touched by darkness, whose light shines straight through the darkness! How blessed we are to be beacons of this light.

Read John 1:6-8. Whom do we meet in the passage? What do we learn about him?

John paved the way for the coming of Christ with the light bestowed on him by the Lord. He knew he was not *the* light but an instrumental witness to it. Like John, we have a responsibility to bear witness to the light of Christ. We live in a lost and dark world that yearns and searches for hope in all the wrong places.

Read Matthew 6:22-23. What is the lamp of the body?

Describe what happens when the eye is healthy.

The Greek word for "healthy," *haplous*, translates to "simple" or "single." The implication here is that when the eye is healthy, its vision is sharp and clear rather than doubled and blurred.

Describe what happens when the eye is bad.

The Greek word for unhealthy, *poneros*, translates to "evil." Jesus' use of it here implies inner darkness and the lack of Jesus' light. It is no wonder Jesus proceeds to say, "If then the light in you is darkness, how great is the darkness!" (Matthew 6:23).

Jesus sandwiches His reminder of the eye being the lamp of the body between two very important passages. Let's take a look at them.

Read verses 19-21. What does Jesus warn against?

Reread verse 21. What is the reason for Jesus' warning?

Lasting Treasure

All too often, I am tempted to believe the transient treasures of this world will satisfy me. That their promise to deliver what I am looking for is exactly what I need. But the truth is, the promises of transient treasures will always come up empty.

The treasures of this world do not last. They can be replaced, destroyed, or stolen. They do not satisfy. They lose their shine. Most importantly, they hold no eternal value.

Storing up the treasures of this world in our hearts—the things we idolize and value more than the Lord (money, comfort, free time, material possessions, etc.)—will only feed our sin and corrupt us. The more we pursue these things, the more we will be pulled away from our yearning for Christ and drawn to ourselves, and the more we will lose sight of our need for Christ and believe we are our own masters.

Sure, the things of this world may hold some earthly value, but they will *never* be more valuable than the One who died the very death we deserve so that we might live. The One who offers us the true treasure of eternal life, light, and love in the heavenly Kingdom that awaits us, a Kingdom that holds more eternal value than our minds could ever comprehend.

As we focus on heavenly treasures, we come to recognize that the value we long to find in the things of this world can be found in Christ alone. What was once extremely appealing starts to lose its shine. These transient treasures become dull, rusted, and meaningless when our eyes are opened to the truth that nothing shines brighter and nothing holds more value than the truest treasure of all, Christ the King.

My dear sister, I implore you to invest in the treasure of the Kingdom of Heaven offered to us in Christ. It cannot be replaced, destroyed, or stolen. Losing everything here on earth would be well worth it in exchange for what awaits us in heaven. Thanks be to God!

The heart wants what we feed it. Take some time to reflect on what currently holds your interests. Transient treasures or Kingdom treasures?

Spend some time in prayer, asking the Lord to identify what your treasure is. How can you store up treasure in heaven and shift your focus to eternal things?

Now let's take a look at the second passage that sandwiches Jesus' description of the eye being the lamp of the body.

Read Matthew 6:24. Describe the two masters mentioned and which one belongs to a healthy eye versus a bad eye.

Can we serve two masters?

We think we can serve two masters, but Jesus makes it clear that our attempts to do so are worthless. Our hearts and service can only belong to one.

It is important to note that the Greek word Jesus uses for "serve," *douleuō*, refers to the work assigned to a slave. The implication here is that a slave belongs to one master. His loyalties cannot be divided.

The same is true for us as Christ's disciples. We cannot serve Him—we cannot shine our light into the darkness—if our devotion belongs to another master, whether that's our career, our wealth, our image, you name it.

In order to serve Christ as our Master, our vision must be clear and set on Him and Him alone.

Describe a time you tried to serve two masters. What happened?

Jesus does not want half-hearted, superficial devotion. He wants every ounce of our devotion. For He alone is worthy of it all! When we serve another master, we rob ourselves of the freedom and fullness of life Christ came to give.

The Lord knows we need Him. This is why He is jealous for us (see Exodus 34:14). He does not—and will not—share the throne with another, for He knows only He satisfies us.

May we know God for who He is and love Him with all that we are (see Colossians 1:16, Matthew 22:37).

Let's put it all together! Read Matthew 6:19-24. What did you learn about light? What are some key takeaways from your reading?

Sound doctrine is important because it affects how we live. It helps us to please our Father in our faith walk. When understood properly, how should Matthew 6:19-24 impact our lives?

Only Jesus is worthy of the throne of your heart. How can you ensure this is the case in your own life?

One Final Charge

> You are the light of the world. A city set on a hill cannot be hidden. Nor do people light a lamp and put it under a basket, but on a stand, and it gives light to all in the house. In the same way, let your light shine before others, so that they may see your good works and give glory to your Father who is in heaven.
>
> MATTHEW 5:14-16

In Christ, we have the great privilege and honor of sharing His light in this dark and hurting world. What a beautiful truth to consider: that God would use us to extend glimpses of Christ's light and love into the lives of others.

We are beacons of the one true hope!

But we must not forget that we cannot keep our lights lit on our own. It is through Jesus, the One who dwelt among us to dispel the darkness of this world, that we are offered the invitation to walk in the light. Second Corinthians 4:6 says that God "has made this light shine in our hearts so we could know the glory of God that is seen in the face of Jesus Christ" (NLT). Knowing this, it is important that we examine ourselves often and tend to the dark and dusty corners in our lives that the light reveals. This way, Christ's light in us can shine from the inside out.

We must be mindful of the treasures we are storing in our hearts to ensure the light that shines from within reflects the truth that we belong to Christ and not the world.

First John 1:6-7 tells us, "If we say we have fellowship with him while we walk in darkness, we lie and do not practice the truth. But if we walk in the light, as he is in the light, we have fellowship with one another, and the blood of Jesus his Son cleanses us from all sin."

To shine the light of truth and life faithfully as daughters of the Most High King, we must walk in step with Him. How do we do this? By reading, studying, knowing, and living out the truths of His holy, infallible Word. For His Word is a lamp for our feet and a light for our path (see Psalm 119:105).

God did not breathe life into your being so that you would dwell in the shadows and blend in with the crowd, my dear sister. God breathed life into you so that you would be set apart; so that you would reflect the glory, light, and love of Christ Jesus; so that you would point those around you to the One above you.

Will everyone understand? Certainly not. In fact, many will criticize and mock you. When this happens, remember that the Lord your God has gone before you and is with you *every* step of the way. The Lord has proven His love for you by sacrificing His one and only Son so that you might be reconciled to Him and able to dwell with Him in eternity. This life is but a breath compared to Christ's coming glory. He is worth the cost!

When the bills pile up, when the doctor delivers unexpected and frightening news, when the media shares one dark report after the next, let us not despair or seek our comfort outside of Christ. Let us instead shine light into these situations with the hope-filled truth and power of King Jesus.

Paul wrote in 2 Corinthians 4:6, "God, who said, 'Let light shine out of darkness,' has shone in our hearts to give the light of the knowledge of the glory of God in the face of Jesus Christ." What does this verse tell us about Jesus as the Light of the World?

Read John 14:7. What do you think Jesus meant when He said if people know Him, they also know His Father?

Make a list of five ways you can practically "let your light shine" in this season of your life. (Hint: Shining your light will not always feel big. In fact, it will likely happen in little but incredibly meaningful ways. For example, it can be as simple as sharing a smile with a stranger in passing.)

For all women who desire to live as daughters of the Most High King, my prayer is that our feet would remain firm on the truths of God's Word so that we would not be disillusioned by the world around us. Instead of letting the world steal our light, may we be bold beacons of the Kingdom light this dark world is searching for. As we delight in God's truth and dwell in the shelter of our holy and mighty God, may the light in us shine brighter and brighter for the whole world to see.

My sister, as we arrive at the end of this session, know this: God loves us *deeply*. So much so that in His love and goodness, He gave His one and only Son so we could be reconciled to Him. He gave us the gift of doctrine so we could grow in our knowledge and understanding of who He is and please Him in our walk. May we rise to the beautiful and bold call of our faithful Father to know His Word and shine His truth and light. As we come to know Him more, may our delight in Him increase. May our joy in the opportunity to carry the hope of Christ into the hopeless places of the world grow all the more as we embrace the call to live as His daughters of delight!

How does pursuing sound doctrine equip us to delight in the Lord?

Describe what delighting in the Lord looks like for you in this season.

Spend time in prayer, asking the Lord to reveal how you can increase your delight in Him and grant you opportunities to faithfully share His Word and shine His light.

Imitate Christ

Recommended Reading: Chapters 4 and 5 of *She Delights*

notes

PREPARING FOR THE SESSION: As you prepare to get started, reflect on and/or discuss the following questions:

- Describe, in your words, what it means to imitate Christ.
- Why is it important for us to imitate Christ?
- How are you imitating Christ in this season of your life?

DURING THE SESSION: Use the space above to jot down notes from Elle's teaching.

TAKEAWAY TIME: What stood out to you most about this session?

PRAY: End your time in prayer, thanking God for the example of Christ's life and the ability we have to imitate Him to the world.

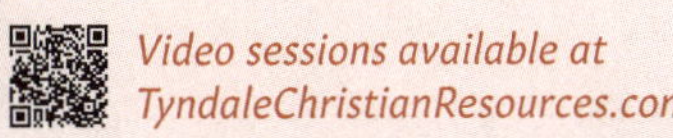

You Are What You Imitate

"I WANT MY WIFE BACK."

I will never forget the day my husband spoke these words to me.

It was a Saturday, and my parents had invited us over to share a meal. When our time together ended and we got back to the car, Michael looked me directly in the eyes and spoke the hard truth I needed to hear.

Once he did so, the whole world went still, and my heart broke into a million little pieces from the powerful plea that fueled his words.

I was miserable. And because I had been unwilling to do anything about it, my husband began to suffer too.

I had convinced myself that I was harboring my misery well—in ways no one could see unless I allowed them to—and that, because the money was good, my twelve-hour days as a nanny of two under two were well worth it.

But I was only fooling myself.

The truth was, we were just two people existing under the same roof during this season, and it was my fault.

But his five words? They changed *everything*.

I knew the Lord was using Michael to give me a much-needed wake-up call. I knew it was time to do something or suffer the consequences.

We spent the forty-minute drive back home processing and discussing what needed to be done while I cried my eyes out and apologized profusely. Michael held my hand, comforted and encouraged me, and told me on repeat that he loved me.

It was a difficult but necessary conversation, and I am so grateful the Lord nudged Michael to call me out. His willingness to do so was an in-the-moment invitation to lay down my pride and let Michael know I could clearly see how I had fallen short in my role as his wife and, most importantly, how my relationship with my Father in heaven was suffering.

All because I had allowed my job to define who I was.

I was so consumed by my work that everything and everyone else around me became exhausting and burdensome—including my marriage and my relationship with God. I had very little energy for anything other than my job.

I had the words of John 3:30—"He must increase, but I must decrease"—backward, and it was time to get my priorities back in their rightful order.

My world began to fall apart from my attempt to center who I was around my work.

In full transparency, I wish this season would not have lasted as long as it did. I wish my marriage did not have to get to the point of suffering in order for me to finally wake up.

But God used it *all* to perform a painful yet powerful work in my heart because, *hallelujah*, He wastes no thing (see Romans 8:28)!

Once my job ended, things began to fall back into place. I began breathing lighter, my joy returned, and I was able to steward my role as a wife—and most importantly, my identity as a daughter of the Most High King—more faithfully.

When I looked in the mirror, I saw a woman whose identity was grounded in her Maker, a woman who was determined to do everything she could, by God's grace, to never again let the world determine her identity, a woman who delights in the truth that her sole obligation is to Christ alone.

This week, we are going to immerse ourselves in Scripture to learn what it looks like to imitate Christ in this modern-day world.

As we prepare to do so, I encourage you to spend time reflecting on the preparation questions at the beginning of this session.

May Christ be magnified through our time studying His Word this week!

DAY 1:

The Goal of Every Christian: Imitating Christ

AS CHRISTIANS, OUR GOAL should be to imitate Christ in all we do.

Often we get so caught up in the hustle and bustle of life that we do not mindfully look for the everyday opportunities to be imitators of our risen Savior.

What would happen, however, if we were to intentionally immerse ourselves in the character of Christ? How might our lives look different? I would love to find out together.

Today we are going to spend time exploring and reflecting on the life of Christ. As we do so, I pray we would grow more eager in our desire and willingness to learn about His character so that we might imitate Him more and more in all we do.

Jesus Was Compassionate

The compassion of Christ should stop us in our tracks. Love and compassion for His people lie at the heart of who Jesus is.

Open your Bible to John 1:14 (ESV) and fill in the blanks:

And the Word became __________ and __________ among us, and we have seen his __________, __________ as of the __________ Son from the Father, full of __________ and __________.

God demonstrated His perfect love for us through the person of Jesus Christ, His one and only Son. Jesus took on flesh and dwelled among us in order to pay the highest price. He *willingly* died the death that we deserved so that we would not have to. Christ the King is the epitome of sacrificial love. Because of His sacrifice, we have been washed clean of our every sin. We have been made new! Jesus made a way for us to be reconciled to our Father in heaven. Death no longer holds the final say. *God* does.

Jesus delighted in responding with compassion to those who suffered. Consider Matthew 15, for example, where we read of a multitude of people who gathered around Jesus to seek His healing.

Take a look at Matthew 15:30-31 and answer the following questions:

What kind of people did the crowd bring with them?

What did Jesus do for these people, and how did they respond?

Jesus did not hesitate at the opportunity to heal those who were suffering. In fact, He had compassion on them.

Now read Matthew 15:32 and answer the following questions:

How long had the crowd been with Jesus at this point?

What was His concern for them?

Now read Matthew 15:33-38.

What do you learn about Jesus' compassion from this story?

Jesus was unwilling to send away the crowd that had been with Him for three days without feeding them. As with the feeding of the five thousand in Matthew 14:13-21, we witness the miraculous. Jesus turns the seven loaves of bread and the few small fish the disciples had on them into enough food to feed the four thousand plus people who made up this particular crowd. In fact, when the disciples picked up the baskets after everyone had had their fill, the baskets were still full!

Jesus could have easily dismissed the crowd without providing food, and they still would have left in awe of the wonders He had performed. But He did not do this. He chose to extend compassion that would prepare them for the journey home.

This is but one example of Jesus' many acts of compassion we read about in Scripture. His compassion demonstrates His sensitivity to fulfill the needs of His people. Jesus' greatest concern, however, is related to our greatest need: a relationship with our Father in heaven. This is why He willingly journeyed to the cross and exuded compassion every step of the way. Because He knew this relationship would be made possible through it. He knew He was the key that would change everything. Praise God!

How have you experienced the compassion of Christ?

How can you show the compassion of Christ to others in your life?

Jesus Was Humble

One of the most beautiful pictures of Christ's humility is found in John 13.

Read John 13:1-11. What did Jesus do?

This unforgettable moment speaks volumes. Jesus knew He was hours away from hanging on the cross. To mark the beginning of the end of His ministry, He washed the feet of His disciples.

Jesus loved His disciples from start to finish. He led them, ate with them, and protected them. He taught them more than they would ever be able to learn from anyone else.

Jesus put His love for the disciples on full display by taking on the role of the lowest servant and washing their feet. Jesus knew His final hour was coming, yet all He desired to focus on was humbling Himself before His disciples.

Write the words of John 13:1 below.

Did you know the Greek for "the end" in this verse is *telos*? It means "unto the completion" and refers to the end of Jesus' earthly life.[1]

Jesus knew that His sacrifice on the cross would accomplish the disciples' salvation. This is how He would love them—us—until the end: by dying the death He did not deserve so we could have eternal life.

Describe how thorough Jesus was in washing the feet of His disciples according to John 13:4-5.

Jesus literally girded Himself with a towel. During this time period, only a bond-slave—someone who was in a position of complete servitude—would have wrapped a towel around himself like this. By girding Himself with a towel, Jesus took on the role of a slave. And not just any slave, but a slave of the lowest order.

What does this scene reveal to you about the humility of Christ?

His willingness to take on a role that was beneath Him confused the disciples, especially Peter, who decided to speak up about it. But Peter could not change what had already been set in motion.

What does Peter tell Jesus in John 13:8?

How does Jesus respond?

After Jesus lovingly reminded Peter to stay in his place, Jesus proceeded to tell His disciples in John 13:14 something we all need to hear.

Read John 13:13-14. What does Jesus say to do in verse 14?

In the space below, reflect on what it means to wash the feet of others.

Jesus humbly took the form of the lowest servant possible in order to demonstrate the depths of His love for His disciples.

As a people who belong to Christ, it is so important to recognize this and extend this same humility to those around us.

Jesus is the embodiment of humility. The account we have of Jesus washing His disciples' feet speaks volumes, but He set an even greater example of humility through His crucifixion. Jesus chose to humble Himself because He knew His obedience was the only way to save us and bring glory to the Father.

Describe the impact Christ's example of humility has had on your life.

What does it mean for us to live from a place of humility with Christ as our example?

Jesus Was Forgiving

In John 8, we read of a woman who was caught in the act of adultery. The religious police—also known as the Pharisees—decided to bring her before Jesus to see how He would respond. They knew exactly where Jesus could be found: at the Temple. This was the most public place in Jerusalem and where Jesus boldly shared and proclaimed His truth for all to hear. The Pharisees were hungry to get rid of Him and did everything they could to achieve just that.

Read John 8:1-11. Describe what happens in the space below.

How would it make you feel if I told you catching this woman in the act of adultery did not take place by happenstance? It was premeditated. The Pharisees were well aware of what was happening and used this as an opportunity to trap Jesus into demonstrating He was not who He claimed to be. Think about it . . . Why was the man not brought before Jesus too?

Not just that, but the rules of the Mosaic law were very strict. For it to apply, there had to be at least two witnesses who agreed, word for word, in their testimony. Adultery is a pretty private sin, is it not?

This was a trap the Pharisees wanted Jesus to walk into, and they did everything they could to ensure its success. In order to catch this woman in the act, they would have had to send spies to lay eyes on what was being done behind closed doors.

What do you think the Pharisees and scribes were implying when they asked Jesus, "What do you say?" (verse 5)? What do you think they wanted Him to say?

Read verses 6-8. How *does* Jesus respond to their test?

I love His response here! Jesus ignored them. Scripture tells us He stooped down and started writing on the ground, in the dust, with His finger. Make no mistake here, my friend. This was a very intentional act on Jesus' part. This act of stooping down showed that Jesus identified with the sinful woman whom the Pharisees and scribes were trying to humiliate. It is not known what Jesus wrote, but we can trust that it was just as intentional as His act of stooping down to identify with this woman.

As the religious leaders continued to press Him, Jesus rose up, looked them in the eye, and responded with exactly what they needed to hear.

Read John 8:7. What does Jesus say?

Rather than addressing the woman caught in adultery, Jesus stood up to establish His authority over the Pharisees and call them out on their own sin. *Mic drop.* Jesus knew this spotlight moment of shame and humiliation had been planned. He knew the religious leaders were trying to use this woman as a weapon against Him in order to disprove His authority. They ended up catching themselves in their own trap.

Picture yourself as a witness to this exchange between the Pharisees and Jesus. How would it make you feel?

Let's explore what happens next.

Read John 8:9. Why do you think the scribes and Pharisees left?

It is likely they left because they were convicted by Jesus' words. Who wouldn't be? They were also probably embarrassed. Jesus accomplished the Father's will in this moment, which was to shift their focus from the woman's sin to their own sin.

Once they leave, Jesus remains with the woman, and a beautiful exchange takes place.

Read John 8:9-11. What does Jesus ask the woman? Why do you think He asks her these things?

This woman's accusers have left the picture. There was only One left who could condemn her, and He chose not to.

As William Barclay puts it, the accusers "knew the thrill of exercising the power to condemn; Jesus knew the thrill of exercising the power to forgive."[2]

Jesus extends His mercy and forgiveness to this woman and ushers her from death to life in Him! This woman was marked by His redemptive touch, and her life would no longer be the same.

Instead of condemning her, Jesus sends her away with a charge to repent and sin no more.

Instead of leaving her shackled to sexual sin, He breaks its bonds and frees her from it, giving her hope for the future.

The reality is that this woman would face consequences for her sin, despite this life-altering encounter with Jesus. She would likely be rejected by her husband and excommunicated from her community. She would not be able to avoid the consequences of her sinful choices, but thanks be to God, this woman would be able to move forward in hope.

This powerful story demonstrates that Jesus came into the world to save us from the condemnation and death our sins deserve. Left to ourselves, we are helpless. But thanks to Christ's intervention, we have a sure and steadfast hope! We have life through Him.

Describe the impact Christ's forgiveness has had on your life.

Do you struggle to forgive others? If so, why do you think that is?

Is there someone in your life you need to forgive? What steps can you take today to move in the direction of forgiveness?

My friend, as we wrap our time up together today, let us rejoice in the truth that Jesus is the perfect example of all the qualities we should exemplify in our personal lives.

There is no one like Him. For He did for us what we could not—*what we could never*—do for ourselves.

Thanks be to God!

DAY 2:

The How of Imitation

TODAY WE ARE GOING TO EXPLORE two powerful ways to imitate Christ. Before we do so, take some time to reflect on the following questions:

What is your most memorable moment of witnessing someone else being Christlike?

What encourages you to imitate Christ?

Deny Self

The concept of self-denial is something this self-driven world will always look down upon. It simply does not make sense to those who walk in the dark. We will be mocked for it. But when we walk in the light, we realize the damage that focusing only on ourselves can cause. As you and I both know, the nature of our flesh is sin. Sin wants us to resist what—*Who*—is truly good for us. Participating in the call of self-denial is not only a good and right thing; it is also a healthy and holy thing! This is why we are called to step away from self-centered living.

In order to be disciples of Jesus, we must live in obedience to the call of self-denial. Our allegiance must be to Christ alone.

Open your Bible to Matthew 16:24-26 (ESV) and fill in the blanks below:

Then Jesus told his disciples, "If anyone would come after me, let him _________ himself and take up his _________ and follow ________. For whoever would save his life will __________ it, but whoever loses his life for my sake will _________ it. For what will it profit a man if he gains the whole ___________ and ___________ his soul? Or what shall a man give in return for his ____________?"

Summarize Jesus' message here in your own words.

Note that the Greek verb used here for *deny—aparneomai*—is the same verb used to describe Peter's denial of knowing Jesus (Matthew 26:69-75).

How does the definition of *deny* help you understand the meaning of self-denial?

Jesus pairs His call to deny self with His charge to pick up our cross. If this does not make you think of Jesus carrying the cross to Calvary, it should. Although He had not yet been crucified, Jesus knew it was coming.

How could Jesus' charge to carry your cross impact your daily life?

Jesus demonstrated ultimate obedience and submission to the Father's will as He carried His cross to Calvary. The call to bear our cross is a call to be wholly submitted to Christ, a call to devote our entire allegiance to Him.

There is no such thing as a half-hearted commitment to the Lord. It's all or nothing. This means we must not simply believe in God in our heads. We must live out our belief by putting His truth on display.

Take some time to prayerfully consider if there is anything in your life that needs to be removed in order to ensure God is your utmost priority.

As we embrace the call to deny ourselves, something truly wonderful happens. We grow in our desire to "fix our eyes on Jesus, the author and perfecter of our faith, who for the joy set before Him endured the cross, scorning its shame, and sat down at the right hand of the throne of God" (Hebrews 12:2, BSB). We care less and less about what the world says and more and more about who Jesus is and how we can imitate Him for the sake of those who walk in the darkness. By choosing to deny ourselves as soon as our feet hit the floor each morning, we are able to savor the true, abundant life—the ultimate freedom—that Christ came to give.

Whatever we may lose as a result of our devotion to our Lord Jesus Christ—our very lives included—we should count as gain because of the eternal reward that awaits. So as we take up our cross and deny ourselves, let us rejoice! For we will not taste death, only glory, because of the way Christ paved to eternal life. Hallelujah!

Behold Christ

To behold someone or something means to fix our eyes upon it. The more we behold a person, the more we become like them. The more we behold a desirable thing, the more we long for it. So let me ask you: What are your eyes fixed on? Money? Comfort? Power? The approval of others?

These are false idols, and they will always be unworthy of worship. Satan knows that when we chase after false idols, we become less concerned with God and more concerned with ourselves. That said, you better believe he is working hard to scheme and distract us from the truth that only Jesus satisfies and completes us.

What are you tempted to fix your eyes on other than Christ?

We are what we worship, and the biblical account of the Israelites shows what can happen when we get this wrong. Second Kings 17:15 tells us, "They despised [God's] statutes and his covenant that he made with their fathers and the warnings that he gave them. They went after false idols and became false, and they followed the nations that were around them, concerning whom the LORD had commanded them that they should not do like them."

Let's take a look at their story.

The Israelites were a self-righteous people who struggled big time to submit to the authority and righteousness of God. The Israelites are a reflection of all of us, apart from God's saving grace in our lives! Even though they witnessed unforgettable displays of God's supernatural power, they remained focused on themselves.

Take the story of the golden calf, for example. When this story takes place, the Israelites had heard God speak on Mount Sinai (see Exodus 20:22) and they had agreed to keep the covenant God had established with them (see Exodus 24:3).

When Moses was on Mount Sinai, God shared many important things with him. God gave him the Ten Commandments, which were accompanied by thunder, lightning, smoke, and the blast of a trumpet to emphasize their significance (see Exodus 20:18-19). In addition, the Lord gave Moses the instructions for how to properly build the Ark of the Covenant, the Tabernacle, the altar, and more (see Exodus 24–31).

While Moses was on the mountain receiving the Lord's instructions, the Israelites began to get impatient. So what did they do? Nothing good.

Take a few minutes to read Exodus 32 and answer the following questions as you do:

What do the Israelites request of Aaron while Moses is on the mountain with the Lord (verse 1)?

Compare Aaron's response (verse 2) to God's response (verse 9).

How does Moses respond to God's anger (verses 11-13)?

When confronted, how does Aaron respond to Moses (verse 24)?

How are the sons of Levi ordained for the service of the Lord (verse 27-29)?

What does God do in verse 35?

If Exodus 32 teaches us anything, it is that there are consequences for our sins—we will ultimately be held accountable for them. Only our sovereign God is worthy of our worship. Worshiping anything else will corrupt us.

So, how are we to worship God wholeheartedly? By beholding Christ, of course!

Read 2 Corinthians 3:17-18 (ESV) and fill in the blanks below:

Now the Lord is the Spirit, and where the Spirit of the Lord is, there is ______________. And we all, with unveiled ____________, beholding the ______________ of the Lord, are being transformed into the same image from one degree of _____________ to another. For this comes from the Lord who is the Spirit.

In the Christian's case, we are to behold Christ above all other things. But we cannot do this—we cannot see and appreciate Jesus for who He is and what that means for us—on our own. In fact, these short but mighty verses tell us that it is only by the power of God's Spirit that we are able to behold Him. The Holy Spirit enables us to understand Scripture so it can change us from the inside out. Praise God!

Let us behold Christ by asking the Spirit to speak to us through the Word and open our eyes to the ways we can live out the truths found within it. Let us behold

Christ by offering our allegiance to Him through self-denial, cherishing His Word, and yielding our hearts to His.

Take some time to pray and give thanks to God for the work of His faithful Spirit in your life today.

As the psalmist so beautifully declares in Psalm 16:8, may the Lord always be set before us. May we look to Christ in order to behold Him with our whole hearts. Amen!

DAY 3:

The Fruit of Imitation

WHEN MY HUSBAND, MICHAEL, and I were engaged, our premarital counselor told us something that has stuck with me ever since.

He said, "Marriage will reveal just how selfish you truly are."

I will never forget this because he was right. Marriage has been a humbling reminder of my own sinfulness.

It has also shown me the importance of abiding in Christ. If I don't do that, the marriage that God intends to be good will not be good.

That said, abiding in Christ is not simply a prerequisite for a covenantal marriage to flourish. It is a call for all Christians—regardless of their marital status—to participate in. Everything we say and do should stem from a place of abiding in the Lord.

Everything.

If we do not abide in Christ, we will become blind to our sin and our spiritual health will weaken—fast. We will rot.

When we abide in Christ, however, we will be equipped to imitate His love, grace, patience, compassion, and so much more in ways God desires. We will bear good fruit!

Today, we are going to study the call to abide and what it looks like lived out. Ready to dive in? Let's do it!

Abide Defined

Read John 15:1-17.

Who is the gardener/vinedresser?

Who is the true vine?

Who is the branch?

In what verse do we find the call to abide in Jesus?

In your own words, describe what it means to abide in Christ.

Jesus offers us this powerful image of a branch and a vine to illustrate what it means to abide in Him. He says, "As the branch cannot bear fruit by itself, unless it abides in the vine, neither can you, unless you abide in me" (John 15:4).

The Greek verb translated as "abide" is *meno*, and it means "remain or continue." The point Jesus is making here is this: only those who remainin Christ can bear healthy and holy fruit.

When you consider this definition, does anything change in your understanding of what it means to abide in Christ? If so, what?

To abide in Christ means to remain in relationship with Him. In order to faithfully abide in Him, we must live in obedience to Scripture. The power of the Holy

Spirit in us is what equips us to obey, and we must not forget this. We also must recall the beautiful truth that when we mess up—and we will—God's grace is enough to cover and carry us through. Everything we do should be done with His present and coming glory in mind, knowing that what we do and the things we endure are woven with purpose and eternal value.

Abiding should be the heart posture of *all* who call on Jesus, the true vine.

Take some time to evaluate the posture of your heart. Is there anything you are struggling to believe about God's character? Are there any lies that might be overshadowing the truth? Ask God to reveal anything that is keeping you from having a submissive heart.

Speaking of the true vine, let's talk about the image of the vine and the branches Jesus uses to illustrate the call to abide: "I am the vine; you are the branches. Whoever abides in me and I in him, he it is that bears much fruit, for apart from me you can do nothing" (John 15:5).

Have you ever seen vines in the wild or on your property? They are pretty to look at, but they sure do spread fast, don't they? Often, vines are seen as an annoyance. In this Scripture passage, however, the vine is a glorious announcement. Jesus referring to Himself as the true vine shows that He is the true source of life—our salvation—who connects us to our great God.

When we, the branches, abide in Christ, the true vine, who abides in God, the gardener, we will bear good fruit. The fruit produced from this vine never goes bad. As we abide in Christ, the gardener will tend to our branch and prune what needs to be removed so that we may more faithfully abide and bear good fruit.

How beautiful is that? As we abide in Christ, we grow and produce righteous, supernatural fruit. Take love, joy, peace, patience, kindness, goodness, faithfulness, gentleness, and self-control, for example (see Galatians 5:22-23)! This fruit is evidence of the indwelling of Christ in us. As we bear this fruit, we bear His image to the world.

Take a look at John 15:3. What does God use as His gardening shears?

What does it mean to be fruitful in Christ? What are some fruitful areas of your life? What are some areas where you could grow in fruitfulness?

Read 2 Peter 1:3-9. What does this passage teach us about being fruitful?

Abiding does not save us; it *sanctifies* us. Our desire to abide is something that comes not from our own doing but as a result of Christ's salvation.

As you pursue the Lord and seek to remain in Him, I pray that God would stir your affection for Him in a way that grows and places your hunger and thirst for Him on full display for all the world to see.

Take some time to reflect on how you can grow and seek God's help in the following areas:

Denying yourself and following Christ's example

Living in the Word and walking in obedience to God's command

Surrounding yourself with those who are like-minded in faith

Choosing actions and words that reflect your love for Christ

Embracing God's grace when you fall short in any of these areas

How to Faithfully Abide

Read John 15:10.

How do we faithfully abide in Jesus?

Simply put, to abide means to know God's Word and to live in obedience to it. To recognize that our true hunger will only ever be satisfied by feasting on the Word. To ask God to use His Word to permeate our mind, redirect the desires of our heart that are not in alignment with His will, and to grow us in our love for serving to Him.

To abide means to rest in the finished work of the Cross and the love that was poured out on us as a result of the greatest sacrifice the world will ever know.

We cannot live as faithful followers of Jesus if we do not abide.

We also cannot do this alone. In order to abide well, we must rely on the power of the Spirit at work in us. For it is the Spirit who sanctifies! It is through God's Spirit in us that we are able to bear good fruit from our belief in Jesus Christ, the true vine.

Abiding in Christ does not mean we won't fall short, because we surely will. But when that happens, we can rejoice because we have the Spirit willing and ready to cover us in grace, prune our hearts of the things that don't belong there, and redirect our gaze back to Him.

When the Father begins to prune you, I encourage you to embrace it. Sure, it may not feel good in the moment, but take heart because it is for His glory and our good. God delights in pruning us so that we might be fruitful imitators of Christ. His pruning is never without purpose. In fact, it points us to the greatest purpose of all: to know Christ and make His name known! Store this truth in your heart, for it is one worth rejoicing in.

If you are interested in further exploring what the Bible says about abiding in Christ, check out John 15:2, Romans 5:3-5, and James 1:2-5.

In the space below, describe a time when you experienced pruning from our faithful Father. What did that experience look like?

What obstacles have you faced when trying to abide in Christ?

Now, let's talk about two powerful ways to faithfully abide in Christ.

Acknowledge Your Need for God's Word

As Christians, we cannot live as if we do not need the Word. If we claim to know the truth but do not actively dwell in Scripture, it won't change us! The Word is what shapes us and grows us in our understanding of who God is. God uses our time in it to fashion us in His glorious image. Draw near to the Lord through His Word and He will meet you there. (See Psalm 119:105; Isaiah 55:11; 2 Timothy 3:16; and Hebrews 4:12.)

Gather with Other Believers

We were created to take part in the body of Christ—to do life with community! It is part of God's good design for our growth and well-being. God loves the church, and so should we. Please do not neglect your need for it. Gather with faithful followers of Christ. Live life together. Rejoice with one another and bear each other's burdens. Edify and encourage each other. Worship together.

In doing so, you will be honoring the Father's good design for His people. Dietrich Bonhoeffer once said, "It is grace, nothing but grace, that we are allowed to live in community with Christian brethren."[1] Enjoy this gift of God's grace!

We are branches of the true vine, sister. Let us rejoice in this beautiful truth and glorify Him in all we do. Let us *abide*!

Are there areas of your life that still need to be pruned? What would it look like for you to submit to the Father in these areas?

What spiritual practices (prayer, fasting, Bible study, church involvement, etc.) help you abide in Christ?

May we stay connected to the true vine by drawing our nourishment, energy, and strength from Christ alone. May we experience the eternal benefit of bearing His righteous and glorious fruit. Amen!

DAY 4:

Remember in Order to Remain

WHEN I WAS GROWING UP, I hated multiple-choice tests. On any given day, I would have preferred to write a ten-page paper on the most boring topic to ever exist than to enter the battlefield of multiple-choice questions.

Sadly, multiple-choice tests were pretty much inevitable as a student. I had to learn how to deal with it. To do so, I trained my brain to memorize as much as it could. I would stuff it full of significant events, dates, and any other information that would be useful testing information.

I usually did pretty well on these tests, but my brain refused to hold on to the overwhelming amount of information I had crammed into its folders. Once one test was over, my brain emptied its folders in order to make room for the next test.

You see, I wasn't actually absorbing the knowledge long-term. I was not choosing to remember the information I memorized because it held little value to me. I was simply holding on to it long enough to pass those exams and surprise pop quizzes.

This method may have worked for me as a student, but it does not work for me as a daughter of the Most High King.

In Christ, we are provided with the knowledge that we are to remember His ways in order to remain or abide in Him. The Holy Spirit within us makes this possible (see John 14:15-18).

Today, we are going to read Ephesians 5:1-20 together and explore what remaining in Christ looks like in everyday life.

Grab your Bible if you have not already done so, and let's dive in!

Becoming an Imitator of God

Read Ephesians 5:1-11 (ESV) and fill in the blanks as you do so:

Therefore be ________________ of God, as beloved children. And walk in __________, as Christ loved us and gave himself up for us, a fragrant offering and sacrifice to God. But _____________ _________________ and all impurity or covetousness must not even be named among _______, as is proper among ____________. Let there be no filthiness nor foolish talk nor crude joking, which are ________ _______ __________, but instead let there be _________________. For you may be sure of this, that everyone who is sexually immoral or impure, or who is covetous (that is, an idolater), has no __________________ in the kingdom of Christ and God. Let no one deceive you with empty words, for because of these things the _____________ of God comes upon the sons of ________________. Therefore do not become ______________ with them; for at one time you were ______________, but now you are ___________ in the Lord. Walk as children of light (for the fruit of light is found in all that is ___________ and ___________ and ___________), and try to discern what is pleasing to the Lord. Take no part in the ______________ works of darkness, but instead _____________ them.

What does it mean to be imitators of God?

What things should we avoid practicing as imitators of Christ?

The Greek word for "imitators" used in Ephesians 5:1 is *mimētēs*, which is related to the English word *mimic*. This word has a positive connotation of trying to be like another. It is used seven times in the New Testament to encourage believers to follow or emulate church leaders, Jesus Christ, and ultimately our great God.

Let His Light Shine

Here is what this means for us: the more we look to the Lord and get to know Him through Scripture, the more exposed we will be to His heart and character. As we spend time in His presence doing these things, God will use it for His glory and our good! Our faithful Father will continue to fashion us in His likeness, and we will be able to imitate Him in the ways we are called to.

I love the way Christian educator and author Lawrence Richards describes it. He says *mimētēs* "is a call to reproduce in our own way of life those godly qualities that result from salvation and that we see in others. The idea is intimately linked with the thought that teachers and leaders ought to be clear, living examples of the practical implications of commitment to Jesus."[1]

In this passage, Paul shares three "walks" necessary in order to imitate God. What are they? (See verses 2, 8, and 15.)

Paul lists specific sins that Christians should abstain from in order to walk in the light of Christ. List the sinful behaviors he includes in verses 3-5.

This Scripture passage encourages us to display the fruits born from walking in the light. What three pieces of advice does Paul provide in verses 7-10?

Paul says believers are to expose the darkness, not participate in it. What effects of shining Christ's light does Paul share in verses 13 and 14?

The final verses of this passage offer a charge for us to walk in wisdom. What does Paul tell us to do in verse 16? How can we do this? (See verses 17-20.)

My friend, there is *no greater blessing* than to experience Christ's light sustaining and guiding us. May we know this, embrace this, and let our light—*His light*—shine! May we imitate His holy ways for all the world to see.

DAY 5:

As I Imitate Christ

"BE IMITATORS OF ME, as I am of Christ" (1 Corinthians 11:1).

Have you ever told anyone this?

My guess is probably not. After all, this is quite a statement, is it not?

The call to imitate Christ is one of the *greatest* honors we have as children of God. Far too often, however, we are tempted to spend our time looking to those who live the type of earthly lifestyle we long for rather than the One who provides the only type of life worth living.

As we wrap up our week of studying the command to imitate Christ in the things we do, let us explore what exactly Paul meant by his words in 1 Corinthians 11:1, and the meaning these words hold for us today. First, take a few moments to answer the question below.

Who is the most godly person in your life? Why?

Faith, Not Perfection

As we consider Paul's words in 1 Corinthians 1:11 and the command to imitate Christ, let us do so with the knowledge that no one can be perfectly like Christ.

Thankfully, though, it is not perfection that is required of us. It is sincere faith in the only One who can make us perfect.

The Christian who is diligent in imitating Christ will have faith in the Lord driven by humility, obedience, and repentance. The Christian who is diligent in imitating Christ will be fueled by God's glory and not her own.

How does the statement Paul makes in 1 Corinthians 11:1 make you feel?

What do you think Paul is implying by his words here?

This statement may unsettle you at first by how daunting it feels. But it shouldn't. And here's why:

When Paul says, "Be imitators of me, as I am of Christ," he means to imitate the good—the Christlikeness—you see in him, which is the same Christlikeness that resides in all who belong to the Lord. Paul knew whom he belonged to. He led a public ministry that was often devoted to reconciliation within the church. This is why he could speak these words to the Corinthian church, not from a place of arrogance and pride, but from the love, joy, and freedom he had in Christ. He knew the Corinthians were struggling and needed a personal example. He also knew Jesus' way of living was the only way to life.

Paul was not saying, "Look to me over Christ." He knew he was far from perfect (see Philippians 3:12-15 and 1 Timothy 1:15). He was shining a light on what Christ had done in him and how he was able to imitate the character of Christ because of the Lord's gracious and miraculous intervention in his life. He was calling the Corinthians not to look to their own strength but to the work of Christ in them so they could imitate Christ in all they did—including the ways they reconciled their differences.

Jesus should always be the One we look to, over anyone else. But as we look to Jesus, we will become living examples to others who follow Jesus as well.

When Christlikeness is the goal, we can invite people to imitate us as we imitate Christ.

Does this change the way you initially understood 1 Corinthians 11:1? If so, how?

We Are What We Imitate

As I write this study, my daughter Selah is almost two years old. As her mother, I want nothing more than for her to know and love the Lord her God with all her heart, mind, and soul—for all the days of her life.

I long for her to imitate the Christlikeness she sees in me. I want her to see and know that Christ is my number one priority. I want her to understand why her father and I have chosen to raise her in His statutes and why the decisions we make are grounded in our identity in Him.

Just as much as I long for these things, however, I must also recognize that Selah will also see my shortcomings—my dirty, rotten sin. The things I struggle to surrender to the Lord—the things I long for no one to see—will be seen by my family.

I do not like this reality. Yet, at the same time, I see the opportunity to set an example of humbling myself before the throne and repenting of my sin at the feet of my Savior.

This desire I have for my children to know that I am a daughter of the Most High King is a desire that requires ongoing change—sanctification—in my heart. It is a change I cannot bring about in myself, a change that requires me to keep my eyes on Christ.

In order to set the example and invite my children to imitate Christ in the ways that I do, I must equip myself. I must read, study, and know God's Word. I must yield my heart to God in such a way that says, "Not my will but Yours be done." I must be diligent in repenting of my sin and asking the Lord to sanctify me so Christ will be magnified in my life and within the walls of my home.

As we look to the example of Christ and become more like Him, others will be able to imitate us—*Christ in us*—and ultimately become more Christlike too.

Look up the following Scripture verses and make a list of the qualities we should imitate as we become more like Christ.

1 Chronicles 16:34

Psalm 20:7

John 13:34

Colossians 3:13

Titus 2:7-8

Which of these qualities are already a regular part of your life, by God's grace?

Which of these qualities could you ask the Lord to help you grow in?

My friend, we are what we imitate.

May we imitate those who imitate Jesus.

May those around us see Christ in us.

Let us imitate our church leaders who devote themselves to beholding God through the studying and teaching of His Word; the women's ministry team who faithfully stewards the role of cultivating Christ-centered community among the women in our church body; the couple who joyfully greets us as we arrive at church on Sunday mornings; the children's minister who recognizes the importance of raising children in the church and equipping families with resources for at-home discipleship; the widow who shows up, despite her grief, in order to worship the Lord with her brothers and sisters in Christ.

As we do, may we, like Paul, confidently invite others to "be imitators of me, as I am of Christ," not because of anything we have done but because of everything Christ has done in us.

Amen, amen, amen.

SESSION 3 VIEWER GUIDE

Hate What Is Evil

Recommended Reading: Chapters 3 and 7 of *She Delights*

notes

PREPARING FOR THE SESSION: As you prepare to get started, reflect on and/or discuss the following questions:

- How do you define evil?
- What lies does Satan most often whisper in your ears?
- How would you describe the difference between worldly hate and biblical hate?
- Why is it important for us to hate the things God hates?

DURING THE SESSION: Use the space above to jot down notes from Elle's teaching.

TAKEAWAY TIME: What stood out to you most about this session?

PRAY: End your time in prayer, thanking God for the example of Christ's life and the ability we have to imitate Him to the world.

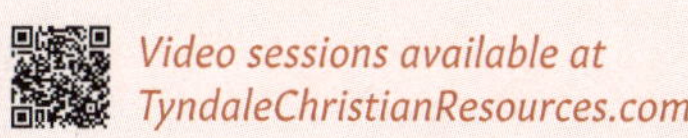

Beware of Fool's Gold

ARE YOU FAMILIAR WITH THE TERM "FOOL'S GOLD"?

On the most basic level, it refers to certain minerals that can easily be mistaken as gold by the untrained eye.

As I was prayerfully preparing the outline for this session, God placed this idea of fool's gold on my heart. When I started looking into this theme, I quickly began to see why.

The United States Geological Survey explains that "fool's gold can be one of three minerals. The most common mineral mistaken for gold is pyrite. Chalcopyrite may also appear gold-like, and weathered mica can mimic gold as well. Compared to actual gold, these minerals will flake, powder, or crumble when poked with a metal point, whereas gold will gouge or indent like soft lead. In addition, actual gold will leave a golden yellow streak when scraped on a piece of unglazed porcelain. Pyrite and chalcopyrite will leave a dark green to black streak and the common micas will leave a white streak."[1]

Is it just me, or do you see the spiritual symbolism here?

Sin is not ugly on the outside. It is alluring. In fact, its deceptive charm played quite the role in the Fall.

To help prepare for our time studying the call to hate what is evil this week, turn to Genesis 3:1-6 (ESV) and fill in the blanks below:

Now the ____________ was more __________ than any other __________ of the field that the LORD God had __________. He said to the woman, "Did God ______________ say, 'You shall not eat of any tree in the garden'?" And the woman said to the serpent, "We may eat of the fruit of the trees in the

______________, but God said, 'You shall not ________ of the fruit of the tree that is in the ___________ of the garden, neither shall you ___________ it, lest you _________.'" But the serpent said to the woman, "You will ________ surely die. For God knows that when you eat of it your eyes will be _______________, and you will be like __________, knowing good and evil." So when the woman __________ that the tree was good for food, and that it was a ______________ to the ______________, and that the tree was to be desired to make one wise, she took of its fruit and ate, and she also gave some to her husband who was with her, and he ate.

Now reflect on the following questions:

What was the motivation behind the serpent's question to Eve in Genesis 3:1?

Why do you think this question was so alluring to Eve?

What was the serpent accusing God of in Genesis 3:4-5?

Want to know something interesting? The most common mineral mistaken for gold is called pyrite. Its name comes from the Greek *pyrites lithos*, which means "the stone which strikes fire."[2]

To humor ourselves with the fool's gold of sin is to play with fire.

Fool's gold holds its shine for but a moment. Then it tarnishes. The gold of God's Kingdom and glory, however, is pure. It never loses its shine, nor will it ever lose its value.

Take the story of Adam and Eve, for example. God gave them everything they needed. They did not go without. Yet the slithering, talking serpent (Satan) tempted Eve to believe that they were, indeed, without. The one rule God gave them—do not eat from the tree of the knowledge of good and evil—was the one thing Satan used to bait Eve into playing with "the stone which strikes fire," into believing that the forbidden fruit was the one thing she needed. And what happened as a result? Humankind became separated from God and plagued by sin, setting into motion our desperate need for a Savior.

This week, my prayer for us is that God would use our time together to train and equip our eyes to recognize fool's gold for what it is: worthless. May we trust that we will find what we need in order to hate what is evil and cling to what is good by looking to our faithful Father as our guide (see Romans 12:9).

DAY 1:

The Battle Within

WHAT IS WRONG WITH ME?

Oh, if I had a dollar for the number of times I have asked myself this question! Surely you can relate?

The internal strife caused by the battle of temptation being waged against us as Christians is weighty, overwhelming, and exhausting, to say the least.

Perhaps you have said something unkind you knew you did not mean, simply because you believed it would make you feel better in the moment.

Maybe you embraced the materialistic belief that some item you lacked would satisfy you in ways it did not after you purchased it.

Perhaps you chose to wrong someone who first wronged you.

Or maybe you entertained a sinful thought instead of dismissing it the second it showed up.

I'm guilty of all these things and more. I have wrestled many times with thoughts like these and wondering if I am truly saved because of the ongoing battle at hand.

If we love the Lord, then why do we continue to fall short?

Thanks be to God, Paul speaks to the root of these questions in Scripture.

I can remember one of the first times I discussed my ongoing battle against sin with my husband, Michael. He referenced Paul's words in Romans 7.

Open your Bible to Romans 7:15-20 (ESV) and fill in the blanks as you read it.

I do ________ understand my own ______________. For I do not do what I ________, but I do the very thing I ________. Now if I do what I do

________ want, I agree with the ________, that it is __________. So now it is no longer I who do it, but _________ that dwells within me. For I know that nothing ___________ dwells in me, that is, in my flesh. For I have the __________ to do what is right, but not the ___________ to carry it out. For I do not do the __________ I want, but the __________ I do not want is what I keep on doing. Now if I do what I do not want, it is no longer I who do it, but ___________ that dwells within me.

What does verse 18 reveal about the flesh?

Describe a time you experienced the reality of our sin nature described in this passage.

Here's the thing, my friend. As believers—no matter how spiritually mature we may consider ourselves—we will always be fighting sin until Christ's return. Always. The difference, however, between our old life outside of Christ and our new life in Christ is that we now share in Christ's victory. So, although we still struggle with sin in this life, it is no longer our identity. It no longer has the final say because it no longer rules and reigns over us. This is not to say our battle with sin gets easier. Sometimes it will feel as if the battle has just begun. But we can rejoice because the source of our sin—our fallenness—is not part of the new life we have embraced in Christ. Christ is now enthroned as the sovereign Lord over our lives. In Christ, we hold victory over our sin. Praise God!

Recognizing Sin

Now read Romans 7:21-25 and answer the following questions:

Where do we delight in the law of the Lord (verse 22)?

Where do we see the law of sin (verse 23)?

How does Paul describe himself in verse 24?

Who will ultimately set us free from our sin (verse 25)?

Sin might be a remaining reality in the life of every believer, but in Christ we are gifted the strength to recognize the problem of sin in order to keep fighting it; the strength to hate evil and to cling to what is good; the strength to keep our eyes on the God who reigns and sustains.

Strength for the Fight

What would it look like to grow in your spiritual walk so you might be strengthened in your fight against sin?

How have you experienced the power of Christ at work in you in the face of temptation and sin?

How do Paul's words in Romans 5:15-17 comfort you?

May we be fueled by the hope offered by the One who went to the cross to put our sin to death for good. May we grow in our desire to hate what is evil—the sin in us and all around us—as God continues to bestow His grace upon us, use us for His glory, and grow us in personal holiness every step of the way.

DAY 2:

Hate What God Hates

GOD HATES EVIL, AND WE SHOULD TOO.

Why?

Simple. Because we are made in His glorious image, we should love the things He loves and hate the things He hates.

And God hates evil.

Today, we are going to explore how we can do this in a way that brings honor to God's name and grows us more and more in our love for the things that are above.

In Romans 12:9, we are charged to "abhor what is evil" and "hold fast to what is good."

To abhor something is to hate it. Paul does not beat around the bush here, and we should not either. We should constantly be turning away from evil and finding ourselves eager to cling to that which is good.

What God Hates

Evil often disguises itself in appealing ways. How have you seen this in your own life? In what ways have you found yourself drawn to it?

Open your Bible to Proverbs 6:16-19. Here you will find a list of the six things God hates and the seven things God detests. List them in the space below.

Why do you think haughty eyes (pride) is the first thing listed?

List out the opposites of the things God hates:

Haughty eyes

Lying tongue

Hands that shed innocent blood

A heart that devises wicked schemes

Feet that are quick to rush to evil

A false witness who speaks lies

A person who stirs up conflict in their community

What God Loves

If God hates the things we see listed in Proverbs 6, it is safe to assume He loves each of their opposites. Thus, if God hates haughty eyes, He loves eyes of humility (see Philippians 2:3). If God hates a lying tongue, He loves a tongue that speaks truth and life (see 1 Thessalonians 5:11). If God hates hands that shed innocent blood, He loves hands that defend the innocent and serve the Lord (see Proverbs 31:8-9). If He hates the heart that devises wicked schemes, He loves the heart of integrity (see Proverbs 4:23). If He hates the feet that rush to evil, He loves the feet that run toward goodness and righteousness (see Hebrews 13:16). If He hates a false witness, He loves a witness who bears truth (see Acts 10:42). If He hates those who stir up conflict in their community, He loves those who work to sow connection, harmony, and peace within the body of Christ (see Ephesians 4:1-6).

The writer of this proverb poses a very important question for us to consider here, and it is this:

What kind of people are we striving to be? Take some time to reflect on this question for yourself.

May we be a people who strive to love the things God loves and hate the things God hates. May we do so by acknowledging, surrendering, and repenting of our sin in order to turn our hearts away from evil and toward the Light.

DAY 3:

The Heart of Our Worship

AS A CHILD, I THOUGHT OF WORSHIP as solely the act of attending church on Sundays. It was not until later in life I began to realize that worship is so much more than church attendance. The beautiful truth about worship is that it is a way of life we are called to in Christ. Whether we are at church, washing the dishes, rising early to meet God in His Word, walking through the valley, feeding the baby at two in the morning, singing in the shower, ministering to a friend, or driving to or from work . . . *everything* we do is an opportunity to turn our hearts toward the Lord and worship Him.

As we center our hearts on the God who is worthy of our every praise, we must be very cautious about the things we fill our hearts with. You've probably heard the saying "We are what we eat." In a similar sense, we are what we worship. This is why we must regularly evaluate the posture of our hearts and ask ourselves what we truly worship.

In your own words, define worship in the space below.

Compare and contrast worldly worship and godly worship.

God does not leave any room for guesswork when it comes to who we are to worship and how we are to worship. In Scripture, He is very clear about the purpose and manner of our worship. Let's consider a few passages together.

The Who of Worship

Read Exodus 20:1-6 (ESV) and fill in the blanks.

God spoke all these words, saying, "I am the LORD ________ God, who brought you out of the land of Egypt, out of the house of slavery. You shall have ______ other gods before ______. You shall not make for yourself a __________ __________, or any likeness of ______________ that is in __________ above, or that is in the __________ beneath, or that is in the __________ under the earth. You shall not ________ __________ to them or serve them, for I the LORD your God am a ____________ God, visiting the iniquity of the fathers on the children to the third and the fourth generation of those who hate me, but showing ____________ ____________ to thousands of those who love me and keep my ________________.

Turn to Isaiah 40:25-26 (ESV) and fill in the blanks.

To whom then will you compare ______, that I should be like ________? says the ________ ________. Lift up your _________ on high and ________: who created these? He who brings out their host by number, calling them all by _________; by the ______________ of his ____________ and because he is __________ in ____________, not _________ is missing.

What do these two passages reveal about the call to worship?

What do these two passages reveal about the posture of your heart?

The How of Worship

Turn to Romans 12:1-2 (ESV) and fill in the blanks.

I appeal to you therefore, brothers, by the ___________ of God, to present your ___________ as a ___________ ______________, ___________ and ______________ to God, which is your _____________ ______________. Do not be ______________ to this world, but be ________________ by the renewal of your mind, that by testing you may ______________ what is the __________ of God, what is ___________ and ______________ and _____________.

These are just a few of the many passages of Scripture that reveal the truth that God detests the worship of anyone or anything other than Himself.

God is the only One worthy of our worship, but the world tells us otherwise. The world says it is okay to worship whatever makes us happy. Manifestation, witchcraft, astrology, sex, money, drugs . . . the list goes on and on.

However, when we worship anything or anyone else but God, we reject Him.

Romans 12:1-2 tells us that, in order to worship the Lord wholeheartedly, we must present our bodies as living sacrifices to Him.

How do we do this? Take a look at the following verses and make note of their instructions:

Matthew 13:20

Luke 9:23

1 Corinthians 6:19-20

James 1:22

1 Peter 2:1

Considering the truths these verses hold, what changes is the Lord leading you to make so that His Word will influence your way of thinking? What steps can you take to allow His Word to rule and reign in your heart?

This, my sister, is worship: hearing and receiving His Word; denying ourselves in order to take up our cross; recognizing our bodies were bought with a price and they are not our own; putting our faith into action; and pursuing holiness.

It is no secret we live in a world that loves to make us happy by giving us what we want, when we want it, but God cares about so much more than a happiness that is contingent on our circumstances. He cares about our holiness and the fullness of His always-accessible joy found within it! And this is news worth rejoicing in!

God cares first and foremost about His glory. His glory will always come first. But the abundant, eternal joy that comes from sharing in His glory is incomparable to any type of short-lived happiness the world may try to offer us. This joy is what God wants His children to experience—*His* joy!

How does it feel to know that your Father in heaven cares about not just your happiness but your holiness?

Describe a time you experienced this truth in your life.

As we seek to center our lives around the One who first loved us, may our lives be a reflection of His goodness and glory. May we tether ourselves to the truths of His Word and reject the false self-saturated ideologies of the world. May we grow in holiness and embrace the gift of drawing near to the Lord through ongoing acts of worship. May we never forget that God alone is worthy of our worship.

DAY 4:

Temptation in the Wilderness

HAVE YOU EVER READ OF JESUS' ENCOUNTER with Satan in the wilderness? There is so much for us to learn from this exchange as we prepare for our battle against evil, and I am eager to dive in with you today!

Open your Bible to Matthew 3:13-17 and answer the following questions:

How does John the Baptist respond to Jesus in verse 14?

What happens in verses 15-16?

What does the voice from heaven say in verse 17?

Jesus' baptism marks the beginning of His earthly ministry. It also takes place right before He is led into the wilderness for a lengthy period of time. This is a powerful event, and its timing is no accident!

Did Jesus need to be baptized? Why or why not?

Jesus' Baptism

John the Baptist knew that there was no need for Jesus to be baptized because He was without sin and had no need for repentance. But John was lacking something essential . . . the understanding that it would be Christ's baptism that secured "all righteousness" for sinners (Matthew 3:15).

Jesus knew baptism was necessary in order to fully identify with His people as the bearer of their sins (see 2 Corinthians 5:21), which would be accomplished in two ways: through His baptism and His death. Jesus' baptism demonstrated His intention to get rid of the great divide sin caused between humanity and God. His removal of our sin was not simply a result of His few excruciating hours on the cross. *Everything* Jesus did during His time here on earth took place with God's glorious and redemptive purpose in mind: that He, the Word, would become flesh and dwell among us for the purpose of defeating sin and reconciling us to God (see John 1:14). Jesus is God's perfect, redemptive plan for humankind. He not only lived aware of this but obeyed God perfectly, every step of the way (see Luke 22:42).

What do you learn about Jesus in 2 Corinthians 5:21?

The life and baptism of Jesus point to His death as a "ransom for many" (Mark 10:45) and show the perfect obedience by which He fulfills all righteousness. Because of this fulfillment, the forgiveness of our sins and the gift of righteousness are possible through our faith in Christ and Christ alone. Jesus made a way for us, and He is the only way.

At the same time that Jesus identified with fallen humanity at His baptism, the Holy Spirit and the Father identified Jesus as the unique Son of God.

Jesus identified with His people through baptism, His anointment with the Spirit, and His victory over evil. Speaking of evil, let's take a look at His exchange with the devil in the wilderness.

Jesus' Temptation

Read Matthew 4:1-11 and list the three ways Satan tempted Jesus.

How did Jesus respond to each of Satan's temptations?

How did Jesus dismiss Satan in verse 10?

Knowing that Jesus spent forty days of solitude without eating anything may have you wondering, *Why would the Son of God go without?*

Jesus went without to demonstrate that He did not owe allegiance to anyone or anything aside from His Father in heaven.

Naturally, after spending such a long time in the wilderness, Jesus was hungry.

Satan knew this and saw an opportunity to strike. But Jesus knew, as John 4:34 tells us, that His food was to do the will of the One who sent Him. His physical appetite was significant, but it was inferior to His appetite for God.

As Jesus stood in the trenches of temptation, He identified with His people all the more. Each time Satan extended an invitation to sin, Jesus responded with the Word of God! He refused to abandon His trust in God. He believed that the Lord would provide. Although Jesus was physically famished in the midst of temptation, He was filled spiritually.

As you read this story, did you notice anything about your own response to temptation?

How can you equip yourself to fight with the weapon of God's Word the next time temptation lurks?

The best way to hate what is evil is to know God's Word and live in accordance with it.

Like Jesus, may we refuse to follow any path other than the path of the cross. May we rely on the sword of the Spirit—*Scripture*—for victory in our spiritual struggles. May we hate what is evil and refuse to abandon our trust in God. May we succeed in our combat with the enemy!

DAY 5:
Armor Up

AS WE WRAP UP OUR TIME TOGETHER exploring what it looks like to hate what is evil, I want to leave you with two words:

Armor up.

We find a powerful charge to do just that in Ephesians 6:10-18:

> Be strong in the Lord and in the strength of his might. Put on the whole armor of God, that you may be able to stand against the schemes of the devil. For we do not wrestle against flesh and blood, but against the rulers, against the authorities, against the cosmic powers over this present darkness, against the spiritual forces of evil in the heavenly places. Therefore take up the whole armor of God, that you may be able to withstand in the evil day, and having done all, to stand firm. Stand therefore, having fastened on the belt of truth, and having put on the breastplate of righteousness, and, as shoes for your feet, having put on the readiness given by the gospel of peace. In all circumstances take up the shield of faith, with which you can extinguish all the flaming darts of the evil one; and take the helmet of salvation, and the sword of the Spirit, which is the word of God, praying at all times in the Spirit, with all prayer and supplication. To that end, keep alert with all perseverance, making supplication for all the saints.

According to this passage, what do we wrestle against?

List out each piece that makes up the full armor of God.

Which piece is the easiest for you to "put on"? Which piece do you struggle with the most?

Preparing for Spiritual Battle

As you and I both know, there is a spiritual war raging between the flesh and the spirit. My prayer is that we would be intentional in remaining aware of this. When we start to lose sight of it, we begin to let our guard down. And make no mistake, Satan will not hesitate to strike when this happens. His only aim is to distract, divide, and destroy the children of God.

First Peter 5:8 tells us to "Be sober-minded; be watchful. Your adversary the devil prowls around like a roaring lion, seeking someone to devour."

Satan would like for us to believe the battle at hand is with our spouses, strangers on social media, the government, and the list goes on. But the truth of the matter is that we are facing a spiritual battle against demons and the dark influence Satan has over so many in this world.

In light of this, how does God desire for us to do battle?

Continuing on, 1 Peter 5:9 tells us to "Resist him, firm in your faith, knowing that the same kinds of suffering are being experienced by your brotherhood throughout the world."

How does 1 Peter 5:9 tell us to resist the devil?

Read Psalm 121:2. What does it tell us?

This is how we fight our battles, my sister. By recognizing that our strength in this fight comes from keeping our eyes, ears, and minds set on our faithful, sovereign Father. This is how we stand firm.

Satan may be powerful, but the Lord our God is *all-powerful.* In Him, we have everything we need for this fight.

As His children, it is our responsibility to armor up not just on Sunday mornings, but every single day.

To pray and speak truth over ourselves, our families and friends, the local church, our communities, and this world . . .

To fill our lives with acts of worship . . .

To live and breathe God's Word in everything we say and do . . .

To be willing to share and spread the gospel every chance we get . . .

To not lose sight of eternity . . .

So that we would remain standing on the battlefield.

How does knowing the gospel help us in the midst of spiritual battle? How does it give us firm footing?

Protection from the Enemy

Armor up, my sister. Put on the belt of truth, the breastplate of righteousness, shoes with the preparation of the gospel of peace, the shield of faith, the helmet of salvation, and the sword of the Spirit.

Which pieces of your armor are strongest? How do you think God desires for you to use those strengths?

Which pieces of your armor are weaker? What steps do you think God desires for you to take with Him to grow in those areas?

Jesus wore this very armor to defeat Satan and secure the ultimate victory. Do you know what that means? It means God supplies us with Himself to fight against the enemy! Take heart in this truth as you stand firm against the devil's schemes and await Christ's coming glory. For when that day arrives, the powerful influence of sin and darkness and the battle we are fighting in this broken world will be no more.

Our great God will crush Satan under our feet (see Romans 16:20). Every knee will bow and every tongue will confess that Jesus Christ is Lord to the glory of God the Father (Isaiah 45:23; Philippians 2:10-11).

May we live our lives and fight this battle in light of the truths of the glorious gospel of our Lord Jesus Christ. As we do so, let us rejoice that God "preserves the lives of his saints" and "delivers them from the hand of the wicked" (Psalm 97:10). He has overcome the world, and He is with us and for us. Hallelujah!

SESSION 4 VIEWER GUIDE

Spread the Gospel

Recommended Reading: Chapters 8 and 10 of *She Delights*

notes

PREPARING FOR THE SESSION: As you prepare to get started, reflect on and/or discuss the following questions:

- How would you define bold faith?
- When you think about bold faith, what stories from the Bible come to mind?
- Talk about a time you were bold in your faith or witnessed someone who was.

DURING THE SESSION: Use the space above to jot down notes from Elle's teaching.

TAKEAWAY TIME: What stood out to you most about this session?

PRAY: End your time in prayer, thanking God for the gift of His Word!

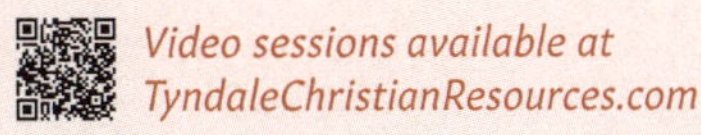

When the Truth Doesn't Feel Good

I'M THE KIND OF FRIEND who refuses to watch you sin and not say something.

If you are living in sin, or if you do or say something that I believe does not honor the Lord, I'm going to do my best not to let it pass, no matter how uncomfortable it might make me, but to instead speak the truth in love.

By no means do I have this down pat, but I am trying.

Because I love you, but I love your soul more.

And I hope and pray you would do the same for me.

Many Christ-centered friendships are not like this. By "this," I mean so rooted and grounded in gospel truth that bold faith and the desire to edify one another and point each other to Christ come naturally.

Several years ago, I discovered something about a close friend that she had not told me. It slipped off the lips of a mutual friend of ours because she simply assumed I already knew.

"Wait, what?" I replied.

"You mean you didn't know?" she asked, "Huh. Maybe she didn't tell you because she knew you would call her out on it."

This mutual friend was not wrong. I would have said something. Because I am "that" friend.

Not because I thought I was better or less sin-filled than she was.

Not because I wanted her to feel bad.

But because I love her and I care about the condition of her soul.

Because I desired to see her walk not in the shame and isolation sin carries with it, but in the forgiveness and freedom from sin that Christ offers us.

I remember talking to Michael about this because my feelings had been hurt. "Why wouldn't she tell me?" I asked.

"Because you are bold," he said, "She knows you will tell her what she doesn't want to hear . . . what she *already* knows."

In full transparency here, the weight of his words made me feel like a bad friend. The reality, however, is that the truth of the gospel offends the flesh. And my friend knew I would carry the truth of the gospel into our conversation, had she shared with me.

I don't like being called out on my sin. No one does. But just because we do not like something does not mean it isn't good for us. Being held accountable is one of the greatest gifts we have in the body of Christ.

God's truth may not always feel good, but it is always *for* our good.

As a people who belong to the Lord, we should always be willing and ready to preach the gospel—to ourselves and those around us.

This, my friend, is bold faith.

Scripture reveals that boldness can be expressed in many ways. During our time together this week, we are going to take a look at what, exactly, bold faith is, where it comes from, what the Holy Spirit's role is in it, and how we can implement it. We will also reflect on the risk versus the reward of living our faith out loud.

I look forward to what the coming days hold. May the Lord use our time together to grow us in our faith and in our desire to live boldly and preach the gospel for His name's sake, for all eternity!

DAY 1:

Boldness Embodied

IF WE WERE STUDYING SCRIPTURE TOGETHER and you asked me to define bold faith, I would word it like this:

> Bold faith is when we act by the power of the Holy Spirit on an urgent conviction. It's moving past how we *feel* about a situation and trusting that following through on our conviction to move will bring glory to God—*no matter the outcome*. It's claiming in *clear terms* who Jesus is and what He has done for us. It is trusting that He is more than able to do something, and that His plan for us is for our good, even if He chooses not to do what we think He should do.

Boldness is a *beautiful* thing, but it often comes with a risk and a cost. The boldness of Christ Himself made it possible for us to be bold too.

How would you describe the difference between biblical boldness and worldly boldness?

Worldly Boldness versus Biblical Boldness

Worldly boldness is driven by self-glory, not really caring about the risk as long as you achieve the thing that makes you feel better and more empowered in the end.

Biblical boldness is being fueled by God's glory and truth, trusting that following Him is the right thing to do, despite the risk. It is suffering for Christ with joy and gladness. It is speaking up even if you stand out in an uncomfortable way. It is choosing to shine the light of God's truth into your heart in the moments you are tempted to sit and stay in your feelings. It is loving God's Word so much that you desire to see it transform those around you. It is standing firm in your faith despite the countless false ideologies the world throws our way. It is embracing the cost of following Christ, knowing that He is worth it all.

This is biblical boldness: that Jesus would knowingly—*willingly*—die the death we deserved so we would not have to face the wrath of God.

Jesus is the embodiment of what it means to be bold. Because we belong to Him, we get to share in this boldness. Because He boldly went to the cross, we can approach the throne of grace with boldness and confidence (see Hebrews 4:16).

In what ways do you desire to be bold like Christ?

Describe a time you embraced the call to be bold or witnessed someone who did.

When we read of Jesus, we learn pretty quickly He was not one to hold back, and rightfully so. He was bold from the moment His ministry began to the moment His life on earth ended.

Throughout the New Testament, we read of the Pharisees' rejection of Jesus. At the root of their opposition was fear. They did everything in their power to diminish His authority and get rid of Him.

In Matthew 12:1-8 we read of an encounter between Jesus, his disciples, and the Pharisees. Read through this passage and answer the following questions as you do so:

What do the Pharisees accuse Jesus' disciples of in verse 2?

How does Jesus respond to them in verses 6-8? What two examples does He share in this passage?

How do you think the Pharisees felt upon hearing His bold reply?

The Pharisees were wrong in their accusation of the disciples violating the Sabbath. Old Testament laws forbade harvesting grain on the Sabbath, not picking grain as a means of sustenance (see Leviticus 19:9-10 and Deuteronomy 23:25). In fact, it was customary for farmers to leave grain unharvested on the edge of the fields because, by doing so, travelers and those who would otherwise go without were able to pick it and feed themselves. This is a beautiful reflection of God's compassion . . . something the Pharisees greatly missed the mark on. This is why they got so upset about the disciples plucking grain: because they did not understand the Father's love for His people. They cared more about keeping the law than recognizing that God did not want His people to go hungry on the Sabbath.

Jesus proceeds to use the example of David and his soldiers breaking the law during a time of need to emphasize the point that He and His disciples could do the same if necessary (see 1 Samuel 21:1-6). He then goes on to mention the example of the synagogue priests who work on the Sabbath. He implies that, according to the accusation of the Pharisees, they, too, would be violating the Sabbath.

As one commentator says, the Pharisees "used those traditions to justify lifting principles like sacrifice above principles like mercy, when God would have them do just the opposite."[1]

Jesus' Bold Claim

Who does Jesus claim He is in Matthew 12:6-8?

Jesus' claim that He was greater than the Temple and Lord over the Sabbath—greater than any Old Testament law they observed—would have likely caused the Pharisees to feel utter shock. Jesus did not beat around the bush. He clearly claimed who He was in the presence of the Pharisees. The Pharisees may have refused to recognize Jesus' identity, but He continued to boldly put them in their place and reiterate His divinity—because He knew who He belonged to.

What scares you when you consider being bold? Surrender your fears into the hands of our almighty God today in exchange for His rest.

How might God be leading you to grow in confidence and boldness today?

Boldness may catch others off guard, and it may feel uncomfortable, but it sure is beautiful. And the truth is, the more we embrace bold acts to share the Good News, the better we will become at it. May we ask for it and, like Jesus, willingly embrace the opportunities to preach the gospel that God grants us. In doing so, may we trust that He will give us the wisdom and strength we need. Amen.

DAY 2:
The Role of the Holy Spirit

HAVE YOU EVER BEEN FROZEN WITH FEAR?

I sure have.

When my daughter, Selah, essentially died in my arms the morning of Black Friday in November 2021, I froze. Before I knew it, I was standing in the back of our hospital room while a large crowd of nurses and doctors surrounded her and rushed her back to the pediatric cardiology ICU to attempt to save her life.

Not knowing what would happen to our little girl, Michael and I watched them roll her away as fast as they could while we remained behind. All we could do was fall to the floor in heartache as we began to plead for her life and, no matter how hard it was, utter the words, "Thy will be done."

After two rounds of nearly perfect CPR that required a group of people working for thirty-plus minutes until they could get Selah hooked up to ECMO, we discovered she was going to need another immediate open-heart surgery to resolve the root of the issue that resulted in her near-death experience.

I will never forget how I felt on this day. *Never.* Externally, I was doing all the right things. Praying, crying, asking for prayers from others, and getting family to come and surround us. Internally, however, it was a different story. I was screaming while staring at the roaring waters of fear that extended an invitation for me to step in and sink down rather than turn my gaze from the storm and place my hope and trust in the only One who could calm it.

Describe a time when you were fearful. What did you do?

Ultimately, by the power of the Holy Spirit, I knew that no matter how much I wanted to give in to fear, I needed to take the hand of the One who was with me in the moment—just as much as He was with the medical staff and my darling Selah. *His* darling Selah. To trust that He saw what I could not. To surrender and let go of the fear that was working overtime to overcome me. To choose faith over fear. To rest in the solace of the One who authors our stories and sees the bigger picture in ways we cannot.

Throughout our stay in the hospital, the Holy Spirit convicted and corrected my mind and heart and pointed me back to Christ. When I was tempted to see only darkness, He opened my eyes to light. When I questioned if God really worked miracles, I witnessed one after the next in the life of our precious girl. God was there and He was moving. No matter the outcome, I knew this and found more comfort than I expected. I would control what I could and surrender what I could not. I would choose faith. Bold, believing faith.

The Bold Disciple

A perfect example of living by fear is found in the life of Peter. Peter was one of Jesus' twelve disciples. If you are familiar with him, you likely know he was sometimes too quick to act and speak. But Jesus loved him, and Peter spent three years as His disciple and close companion. When we find Jesus on trial before His crucifixion, however, we also find Peter denying that he ever knew Jesus—not once, not twice, but three times (see Luke 22:54-62).

At the root of Peter's denial is fear. In the space below, take a moment to reflect on how you can relate to Peter.

Several weeks after Peter's denial and Jesus' crucifixion and resurrection, everything about Peter changes . . . in a good way. A bold way.

In Acts 3, we find Peter and John healing a lame man at the Temple gate. A crowd gathers around them in amazement at what they had done, and Peter boldly tells the people all about the One responsible for the healing they had witnessed—Jesus Christ.

Now turn to Acts 4 and answer the following questions as you read verses 1-31.

What happens to Peter and John (verse 3)?

What does Peter boldly tell the rulers, elders, and scribes, and how do they respond (verses 12-14)?

What do those who surround Peter and John pray over them (verse 29)?

What do you think changed in Peter?

Have you experienced this same change in yourself? What has that looked like in your life?

Peter was filled with the power of the Holy Spirit! In fact, his boldness got him arrested—which was initially the very thing that terrified him to preach the gospel. Fear no longer held him captive once he experienced Jesus' restoration and forgiveness.

In Acts 4:13, we learn that Peter and John's boldness *astonished* the Jewish authorities, and as a result they "recognized that they had been with Jesus." Something interesting to note here is that the authorities recognized who Jesus was, yet they still rejected Him.

Once Peter and John were released, they told the church of the threats they received. These threats likely involved more persecution and even death. They were meant to instill fear so that the disciples would stop preaching the Good News.

Will We Flee or Stand Firm?

What would your initial reaction be to receiving a threat as a result of sharing your faith?

Many of us would be tempted to flee. This would certainly be the easy thing to do, but it would also mean rejecting Christ.

Thanks be to God, the early church stood firm on their Foundation in the face of threats. They approached the throne of God to pray for boldness, and God delivered!

Do you pray for bold faith? Why or why not?

What would it look like for you to stand firm on your Foundation?

As an answer to the believers' prayers, the Lord replaced their fears with His boldness so they could continue to confidently proclaim His truth. They counted the cost and rejoiced in it.

How might the Holy Spirit be stirring your heart toward boldness?

If you are struggling to overcome fear, let me encourage you with its remedy today:

- Spend time in the presence of God. Pray, listen, be still, and know.
- Saturate your heart in the truths of His Word.
- Memorize Scripture and speak it over yourself, your family, and your home.
- Surrender to the guiding power of the Holy Spirit inside you.

When we commit to prioritizing these things and remaining consistent in them, the fear will flee, the fruit will flow, and the boldness will be sure to follow.

Like the early church, may we ask the Lord to "grant to your servants to continue to speak your word with all boldness" (Acts 4:29). May fear not be what grips our hearts but rather all-believing faith granted to us by the gracious, authoritative power of Christ in us!

DAY 3:

When Boldness Leads to the Miraculous

IN MARK 5, WE FIND TWO STORIES of desperate people with bold faith. Let's get to know them.

Open your Bible to Mark 5:21-43. After you read this passage, make a list of the key events.

Aren't these stories *amazing*? In both cases, boldness resulted in the miraculous healing of Jesus' touch! Let's explore Jairus's and the unnamed woman's approach to getting the attention of Christ.

A Sincere Act of Faith

What are some things that stand out to you about Jairus? List them below.

It is important to keep in mind that Jairus was a ruler of the synagogue. This likely meant he was a Pharisee (Jewish religious leader). Scripture tells us many Pharisees did not like or follow Jesus. In fact, they lived in constant frustration at Jesus' teaching of things that were very different from what they were taught.

But Jairus was different. He not only ventured to find Jesus himself; he openly put his trust in Christ by falling at His feet for all to see. This was a *sincere* act of faith on Jairus's part. Unlike most Pharisees, He believed Jesus was who He said He was.

Mark 5:21 tells us Jesus had been teaching on the other side of the Sea of Galilee. Jairus knew He needed Jesus to heal his daughter, and fast. When people heard that Jesus was on His way back, they crowded at the shoreline—and Jairus was part of this crowd.

Imagine falling at the feet of Jesus, begging for your dying daughter to be healed in front of *many* people. Jairus knew all eyes would be on him, a synagogue ruler, but he did not care. He was certain that Jesus was able to heal his little girl, and his boldness drove him to plead that He would do just that. His boldness set him apart.

What I love so much about this encounter is that Jesus acknowledges Jairus's faith by immediately agreeing to go with him to heal his daughter.

The Unnamed Woman

Shortly after Jesus agrees to go with Jairus, Mark introduces us to an unnamed woman with a long-term bleeding issue.

What are some things that stand out to you about the unnamed woman? List them below.

What do the unnamed woman and Jairus have in common?

This woman had suffered for twelve years and spent everything she had on doctors for answers, only to come up empty-handed. Jewish law declared her to be ceremonially unclean because of her issue, which meant she would not have been allowed to enter the Temple for religious ceremonies. This same law revealed that anything she touched would be made unclean as well (see Leviticus 15:25-27). It is safe to assume this woman felt like an outcast. Unfortunately, after she had tried everything in her power to get better, her problem was only getting worse.

Helpless and nearly hopeless, she was nothing short of desperate to be healed. Having only heard reports of Him, this woman had the faith to surrender her power in order to fully trust in His power and ability to heal her. I love what she says in Mark 5:28: "If I touch even his garments, I will be made well." And so, she bent down and extended her hand for what quickly became a life-changing touch.

In a single breath, Jesus was able to do what an endless number of doctors could not do in those twelve long years.

Why do you think Jesus called the woman forth from the crowd after she had been healed?

I can only imagine how embarrassed this woman was by her ongoing issue. Knowing she would be looked down upon for pushing through the crowd and making others unclean as she made her way to touch Jesus, she tried to do so quietly. However, Jesus decided to bless her and acknowledge her faith before the crowd.

This bold and beautiful exchange reveals Jesus as the fulfillment of the Old Testament laws. Because God now dwelled among men through the person of Jesus, this woman did not make Him unclean; He made her clean!

The Faith of Jairus

How do you think Jairus felt when Jesus took the time to pause and acknowledge this woman?

Once Jesus told this woman her faith had healed her and sent her away in peace, Jairus received a negative report about his daughter. Jesus instantly responded to Jairus, "Do not fear, only believe" (Mark 5:36). How do you think Jairus felt upon hearing these words?

Jairus was likely weary and frustrated by Jesus taking his time with the unnamed woman—then devastated by the news that his daughter had passed away. Jesus sensed Jairus's fear.

Jesus knew fear and faith do not belong together, so He took the time to remind Jairus of that as they continued their walk to his home. Perhaps this is why He chose to publicly acknowledge the bleeding woman's faith too: to grow Jairus in his own faith.

The truth Jesus shines light on here applies to us just as much as it did to Jairus: there is no place for fear in a heart filled with faith.

Faith and fear *do not* go together. How have you been tempted to believe otherwise?

During Jairus's time, it was a customary practice to hire professional mourners to grieve when someone died. These were the people who made up the crowd in Jairus's home. Based on how quickly they turned from grieving to mockery, it is obvious none of them had a personal relationship with this little girl and they were only there to grieve superficially.

Jesus refused to entertain the unbelieving crowd and kicked them out, leaving only Jairus, Jairus's wife, and his closest disciples—Peter, James, and John—to witness the miraculous. In a single breath, He spoke life back into the little girl's body, and she rose from the dead.

Read the words of Job 34:19. What does this verse tell us about Jesus and His response to Jairus and the unnamed woman?

Jesus chose to publicly heal the woman who secretly sought His healing, whereas He chose to turn the crowd away and heal Jairus's daughter in private. Why do you think He did that?

How do these two stories show that Jesus is trustworthy?

How do these passages encourage and challenge you to trust Jesus more in your everyday life?

Precious sister, let us not forget that it is only when we place our trust in Jesus that we find the courage bold faith requires. As we learn to trust Him more, like Jairus and the unnamed woman, may our boldness increase and our eyes be opened to the working of our great God and how He desires to use us during our time here on earth. May we be overcome by such awe and wonder for the One who is matchless and glorious in all His ways!

DAY 4:

The Key to Unlocking Bold Faith

IF I WERE TO ASK YOU TO DESCRIBE what it felt like when the Holy Spirit entered your heart and removed the scales from your eyes, what would you say?

I am not the kind of person who has a dramatic testimony—I grew up in the church but did not come to truly know God until He transformed my heart in late high school—but I will never forget what it was like to experience the liberating power of Christ in me.

I could not stop smiling, and all I wanted to do was tell people about the work God had performed in my heart.

When I think of bold faith, I think about that feeling. About experiencing liberation and desiring for people to know this freedom and be changed by it like I had been. About caring more about sharing Christ than what people thought of me.

As I have matured in the faith, I have come to learn that acts of boldness are not meant to be fueled by our feelings. As much as I would love to tell you the excitement of sharing Christ every chance you get never goes away, it just might. Perhaps it already has. If we allow our feelings to determine whether or not we share the gospel, we are going to miss out on so many opportunities to be vessels of God's truth. This is why it is important for us to recognize that we must be fueled by the Father's glory—not our feelings—when we're presented with opportunities to be bold. This is not to say we should not pray for an eager excitement. We absolutely should. But God is worth sharing about even when our feelings try to lead us away from doing so.

Today, we are going to spend time getting to know a woman who had a poor reputation but experienced a powerful transformation that resulted in a beautiful act of boldness.

An Act of Bold Faith

Open your Bible to John 4. Read John 4:5-42 and answer the following questions:

What does Jesus ask the Samaritan woman, and how does she respond (verses 7-9)?

How does Jesus describe the water He offers others in verse 14?

What does Jesus clarify for the Samaritan woman in verse 26?

What does the Samaritan woman do in verses 28-29?

Skip down to verses 39-42. What do we learn?

Here are some important things for us to note about this encounter:

- The time of day. It was very hot at midday. Women usually approached the well earlier in the morning and in groups. The Samaritan woman, however, did not. Either she had an urgent need for water or she desired to avoid running into others who would look at her and only see her poor reputation.

- The societal context. During this time, women were considered property. Only a man could propose to and divorce a woman. Scripture does not clarify the reasoning for her five husbands. Perhaps it was due to barrenness, commitment issues, and/or husband(s) who had passed away.

Upon her arrival, the woman was surprised to encounter a man—a Jewish man, no less—who started a conversation with her. Surprised by Jesus' acknowledgment of her and request for water—Jews did not usually interact with Samaritans—the Samaritan woman fetched water for Him. In return, Jesus extended the most amazing invitation: an invitation to satisfy the thirst in her soul with water from the living Well—the true Christ!

Prior to her encounter with Jesus, the Samaritan woman was drinking from dry wells. Dry wells only lead to one thing: *death*. In order to spiritually flourish, and in order to grow in our boldness, we must drink from the Well that provides the sustenance and transformation our souls crave . . . the Well that never runs dry.

Drink Deeply

I cannot tell you how many times I have been disappointed in my lack of spiritual growth, only to realize it was because I was drinking from dry wells. I was trying to quench my thirst with everything but the Lord and His Word: books, social media, materialism, you name it. I was not being a faithful steward of my time. Nor was I prioritizing my relationship with God. And I was suffering the consequences for it.

What we rely on to quench our inner thirst is a great indicator of how we are doing spiritually. So let me ask you . . .

What well are you drinking from to quench your inner thirst?

When have you struggled to believe Jesus is the Well that never runs dry?

How can you identify with the Samaritan woman?

Filled with Jesus' acceptance and realizing she had found someone who could fulfill her deepest longings, the Samaritan woman ran to others in her town to spread the Good News.

This woman, who was likely marginalized by many, was so transformed by her encounter with Christ that she could not help but share about it. After her exchange with Jesus at the well, the woman proceeded to boldly tell of her encounter with Him for all to hear . . . and the townspeople took her at her word!

This, my sister, is the beginning of bold faith: that we would drink from and depend on the Well that never runs dry to supply our every need.

Have you ever been tempted to believe God could not use you because of how you've sinned in the past? How does hearing the example of the woman at the well—someone God powerfully used despite her sin—give you hope?

Are there any "secret sins" keeping you from drinking from the living Well?

Despite this woman's reputation, many Samaritans believed in Jesus as the Messiah because of what Christ did in her life.

After embracing Jesus' invitation to drink of His living water, the Samaritan woman was freed from the shackles of the sin that held her captive. She no longer cared about what people thought. She now cared about showing them how to experience the freedom she had just stepped into by knowing—*embracing*—the Messiah. Praise God!

Where—or with whom—might God want you to share your testimony in this season?

In what ways does the Samaritan woman's story make you thirst for boldness?

My sister, may we drink *deeply* from the Well that never runs dry! May we approach the Well of God's Word each and every day to drink deeply of the only One who satisfies. May the fruit of our time at the Well enable us to boldly "walk by the Spirit, and . . . not gratify the desires of the flesh" (Galatians 5:16). May we grow in our boldness as we seek to quench our thirst with living water. For when we drink from this Well, we will never thirst again. May we know this and rejoice in it for all our days.

DAY 5:

Faithful Living in a Faithless World

IT IS NO SECRET we live in a modern-day Babylon.

One look at the news will tell you all you need to know to confirm this reality.

This world is a dark and scary place, but in Christ we need not fear.

Easier said than done, I know. But it can—*and should*—be done.

When the flesh is anxious and fearful, the last thing it wants is for us to surrender our weighty feelings to obtain a greater trust in the God of all creation. When I find myself in this place, I am tempted to believe the answers my anxious heart wants are found outside of my assurance in Christ. But Christ's assurance should be the very first thing we cling to! All the answers—whether we come to know them in this life or not—are held in the hands of the One who also holds us. It is *all* in His sovereign hands. We may not know what tomorrow holds, but our eternal, unchanging God does. And because we belong to Him, regardless of what happens tomorrow, we can rest. For we know where we are headed.

How do you struggle to choose faith over fear when you are reminded of how dark and broken the world is?

Living Boldly in Babylon

To wrap up our time studying bold faith this week, we are going to hang out in the book of Daniel. Daniel is a great example of what it looks like to walk in boldness and faithfulness while being immersed in a culture that does not honor God. The book of Daniel can serve as a manual for faithful living in modern-day Babylon.

In Daniel 1, we discover that King Nebuchadnezzar of Babylon has conquered Jerusalem. We are then introduced to a group of four Hebrew exiles who were taken to be immersed and trained in Babylonian culture and literature. Their names are Daniel, Hananiah, Mishael, and Azariah.

As soon as these men entered the king's palace, the chief of the eunuchs, who oversaw their training, changed each of their names.

- Daniel, meaning "God my judge," was named Belteshazzar, meaning "Bel's prince."
- Hananiah, meaning "whom Jehovah hath favored," was named Shadrach, meaning "illumined by sun god."
- Mishael, meaning "Who is what God is?," was named Meshach, after the Babylonian goddess of love and mirth, Shach.
- Azariah, meaning, "whom Jehovah helps," was named Abednego, meaning, "servant of Nego."[1]

All four of these young men originally held powerful names that indicated their belonging and devotion to God. After entering into Babylon captivity, however, they were given new names that referenced Babylonian gods. The purpose of their name change was to encourage them to leave behind the God they knew, to look to King Nebuchadnezzar for their needs instead.

Despite the fact that they were stripped of their names, however, they were not stripped of their faith. They would not leave their God behind.

Daniel and his friends walked in bold faith, and there is so much for us to learn from their witness.

Read Daniel 1:8-21 and describe Daniel's act of courage.

What do we learn in verse 15?

How does the Lord bless these men (verse 17)?

What does the king discover about these men (verses 19-20)?

Right off the bat, Daniel defends his faith and the faith of his friends. It is likely the food these young men were offered was first offered to idols. This is why Daniel requests a simple diet of vegetables and water: so that what they put in their bodies does not go against Scripture. Verse 15 tells us that the Lord blessed and honored this act of bold faith. Daniel and his friends had eaten less than all the other men who were fed by the king, but they looked healthier and more nourished at the end of the trial period Daniel had requested. Not only that, but God also granted them supernatural wisdom and understanding, and He gave Daniel the ability to interpret visions and dreams, which would soon come in handy.

As Daniel and his friends journeyed through their time in the royal service, they had to decide what parts of the Babylonian culture they would embrace and what parts they would reject. How do you do this in today's culture?

A Bold Confession

In Daniel 3, Nebuchadnezzar made a statue of himself that measured ninety feet tall and ninety feet wide. He planned to force everyone to worship it—to worship him. Shadrach, Meshach, and Abednego refused to do so, and the king found out.

How did Shadrach, Meshach, and Abednego respond when the king confronted them about their refusal to worship the statue in Daniel 3:16-18?

This right here is the confession of the bold! Imagine a raging king is demanding your worship, and you tell him you refuse to worship anyone but the God whom you serve. The young men were fully committed to the sovereign Lord, even if He allowed them to burn in the furnace. They would rather have died for their faith than worship someone other than God.

Daniel faced a similar situation in chapter 6. Under the reign of King Darius the

Mede, a temporary law was passed that required the people to pray only to King Darius for thirty days. If anyone refused, they would be tossed into the lions' den.

Read Daniel 6:10. What did Daniel do after hearing of this law?

What was the king's initial response in Daniel 6:14?

Like Shadrach, Meshach, and Abednego, Daniel was miraculously spared by God, who left him untouched by the lions.

Daniel 6:10 tells us Daniel prayed to God multiple times a day, every day. Daniel didn't just know who God was; he knew God intimately. He didn't simply believe in God; he trusted God was who He said He was.

How does Daniel's faith show the importance of maintaining spiritual disciplines in order to grow in our confidence and boldness?

When we read the book of Daniel, we are reminded there are two kingdoms in this world and we are to serve only one of them: the Kingdom of Heaven.

Daniel and his friends experienced the truth that our transforming faith in our everlasting God is what carries us through challenging times. The kingdoms of this world will come and go, but the Kingdom of our great God will be established forever and ever.

This is the Kingdom we belong to.

Does your life currently reflect your commitment to Christ? If not, what needs to change so that it does?

As we look to grow in our boldness for the sake of Christ, let us do two things. Let us first, like the early church, pray for it (see Acts 4:23-31). Boldness is not a fruit of the Spirit. It is not something we are always going to be able to whip out of our back pocket. That said, we can trust that as we pray and look to God, He will be faithful to provide us with exactly what we need in the moments we need it, in order to further His Kingdom and glorify His holy name.

Second, let us deny ourselves (see Luke 9:23). Sin wants us to resist what is truly good for us; to cower away in fear rather than step out in bold faith. Denying self is a good and right thing because it enables us to "fix our eyes on Jesus, the author and perfecter of our faith, who for the joy set before Him endured the cross, scorning its shame, and sat down at the right hand of the throne of God" (Hebrews 12:2, BSB). In Christ, we have everything we need. May this truth drive our bold faith forward.

My sister, when we follow Jesus, we will suffer for His name's sake. Sit with this truth and embrace it. This is the cost: that we would deny ourselves and the temptations of this world in order to pick up our cross and be bold messengers of the gospel on behalf of the One who took His last breath on the cross with us in mind. And this cost is worth rejoicing in! Ecclesiastes 3:11 tells us God has "set eternity in the human heart" (NIV). This is why we can count it all joy: because this world is not our home and something more beautiful than we could ever possibly imagine is coming.

With that in mind, let us pray that the Lord would help us overcome any unbelief caused by fear. That He would diminish our fear in exchange for bold faith, enabling us to truly believe He has equipped us for every good thing as we seek to spread the truth of His Word wherever He may lead. May we be bold vessels of His eternal truth in modern-day Babylon, with unwavering faith in our unchanging and faithful God. May we go and make disciples, trusting that the Lord our God is with us to the end of the age (see Matthew 28:18-20). Amen!

Four Marks of a Bold Christian

1. Our desire to know, love, and please God according to His Word outweighs our desire to please man.
2. People know who we belong to based on the way we live our lives in reverence to Christ.
3. When we come face-to-face with unexpected hardship, our faith is sustained by the One who remains.
4. We are willing to sacrifice everything we have for the sake of Christ—even our lives if necessary.

SESSION 5 VIEWER GUIDE

Walk in a Manner Worthy

Recommended Reading: Chapters 6 and 9 of *She Delights*

notes

PREPARING FOR THE SESSION: As you prepare to get started, reflect on and/or discuss the following questions:

- How would you describe what it looks like to walk in a manner worthy?
- How has God grown and changed you as you have followed Him?
- Do you believe everything you do holds eternal value? Why or why not?

DURING THE SESSION: Use the space above to jot down notes from Elle's teaching.

TAKEAWAY TIME: What stood out to you most about this session?

PRAY: End your time in prayer, thanking God for the gift that is His Word!

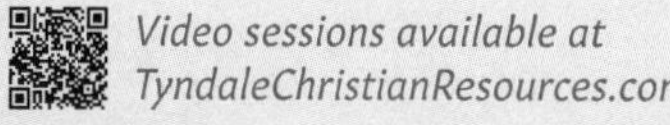

Walk the Walk, Talk the Talk

DURING MY FRESHMAN YEAR OF COLLEGE, I attended an on-campus ministry internship fair, where I interviewed with several churches. I was offered a handful of opportunities that came down to either interning with a youth group at a church in Alabama or with a children's ministry local to me here in Tennessee.

I had listed one of my instrumental high school mentors as a reference. She ended up telling me one of the first questions a church leader had called to ask her about me was, "Is she really that happy?"

I laughed alongside her when she shared that, but internally I felt the heat of embarrassment. I questioned why one of this leader's first thoughts had to do with whether or not I was authentic when I had given her no reason to think otherwise.

I tried to brush off how much it bothered me, but I couldn't. So I took it to the Lord. As I did so, He began to resurface past encounters with others who had also asked how I was able to be so happy all the time. This woman had not been the first to ask, and she would not be the last.

My response to anyone who asked this was always the same: "It's the joy of the Lord!"

After recognizing that people could clearly see how God used me to share His joy with others—whether they actually attributed it to Him or not—I found myself thrilled and thankful that this woman had asked that question. She asked because she witnessed something in me that could only come from Him. As it turned out, I ended up interning under her leadership that summer, so she got to witness my joy in large doses!

As Christians, the words we say and the ways in which we present ourselves matter more than we know. We are called to "walk the walk" and "talk the talk," to conduct ourselves in a way that sets us apart from the world. Although the Bible does not use the exact phrase "Christian walk," Scripture is very clear when it comes to how we should live as we grow in the faith.

The Christian walk is the most blessed and honorable walk there is and will ever be. As daughters of the Most High King, we are called to put this truth on display, to "walk in a manner worthy of the calling to which you have been called" (Ephesians 4:1). So, for the purpose of our final session together, this week we are going to take a deeper look at "walking the walk" and "talking the talk."

As we get ready to dive in, may we be encouraged, challenged, and transformed by the Father's truth. May we grow in our delight of living as the Lord's beloved and ensuring the world knows who we belong to by the way we conduct ourselves. May we walk in His blessed assurance!

DAY 1:
For the Lord, from the Lord

HERE'S THE TEA, SISTER: understanding who we are in Christ is the very foundation of walking worthy.

I grew up thinking it was up to me to become worthy in God's eyes. That if I performed enough acts rooted in faith and love, the Lord would see fit to embrace me as His own.

After I'd lived for years with this misconception, the Lord bent down in His love and grace in order to embrace me as His own, and I realized that His doing so had nothing—*absolutely nothing*—to do with what I could merit on my own.

Read Ephesians 2:8-9. Summarize what it tells you.

Precious sister, our great God has made us worthy *by His grace.*

We know this, but it is easy for us to seek our worth in other places if we are not careful.

Fully Known and Fully Loved

How have you been tempted to place your worth in the hands of something or someone other than God?

Your worth is not found in anything you have done, any titles you have earned, the audience you have gained, or what others think of you. Your worth is found in God's unchanging opinion of you, in your identity as His beloved daughter.

You have been deemed worthy and precious in His sight. And although receiving His favor—His salvation—came at no cost to you, it came at the greatest cost to Jesus: His life.

Your worth is rooted in the most beautiful and sacrificial type of love. Nothing compares to it. You are fully loved and fully known. You can rest secure in this truth.

Do you struggle to believe you are fully known and fully loved? Why or why not?

The command we find in Scripture to walk worthy does not mean we have to earn our position in God's eyes. It means that we are to live our lives in a way that says, "I belong to Christ."

The grace that has made us worthy is the same grace that enables us to walk worthy.

How does this truth meet and encourage you today?

As we prepare our hearts and our minds to walk in a manner worthy together, we must not forget who God says we are.

Spend time resting in the following Scriptures and making note of who God says you are.

- Genesis 1:26-27
- John 15:15
- 1 Corinthians 3:16
- 2 Corinthians 5:17, 21
- 1 John 3:1
- Ephesians 1:4-6; 2:19
- 2 Timothy 1:9

How do these truths differ from what you are tempted to believe about yourself?

Do you believe you are who God says you are? If not, what might be getting in the way?

Why is it important for us as Christians to understand and trust how God views and feels about us?

Precious sister, God has chosen and designed you to live a life that declares His praises. To live as His beloved. The more we embrace who He says we are, the more we grow in our ability to stand unshaken in that truth.

In 2 Timothy, we find a beautiful charge to guard what God has entrusted to us. Paul writes this epistle—or letter—to his young friend and coworker Timothy while imprisoned in Rome and awaiting his approaching death. This is his final exhortation to Timothy, and an unforgettable one at that.

Open your Bible to 2 Timothy 1:8-14 and fill in the blanks as you read through it:

Therefore do not be ______________ of the testimony about our Lord, nor of me his prisoner, but __________ in suffering for the gospel by the power of God, who ___________ us and ___________ us to a __________ calling, not because of our __________ but because of his own ____________ and _________, which he gave us in _________ __________ before the ages began, and which now has been manifested through the ________________ of our Savior Christ Jesus, who ______________ death and brought life and immortality to light through the ____________, for which I was appointed a preacher and apostle and teacher, which is why I ______________ as I do. But I am not ________________, for I know whom I have believed, and I am ________________ that he is able to guard until that day what has been ________________ to me. Follow the ______________ of the ___________ words that you have heard from me, in the _____________ and ____________ that are in Christ Jesus. By the Holy Spirit who dwells within us, ____________ the good deposit ________________ to you.

What is the good deposit Paul refers to in this passage?

The good deposit that was entrusted to Paul and Timothy has also been entrusted to *us*! It is the gospel message, the Christian faith. We guard it by walking in a manner worthy of the calling in Christ that we have received (see Ephesians 4:1); by embracing the call to know Him (see John 17:3) and make His name known (see Acts 20:24); by trusting that our future is secure, even in the midst of our greatest suffering and sorrow (see Romans 8:28); by placing our faith on full display and going to battle with the confidence that it has already been won, because it surely has been (see 1 John 2:14).

But we cannot do this alone . . .

Walking Worthy

According to 2 Timothy 1:14, how is it possible for the Christian to guard the glorious gospel of our Lord Jesus Christ?

Just as we are made worthy by God alone, we are able to walk worthy because of the power of the Holy Spirit in us. The Spirit is the key to our faithfulness.

As we walk in step with the Lord and His will for us in Christ Jesus, we will be able to grow in our ability to walk in a manner worthy of our calling. Praise God!

Friend, live tethered to Christ and find joy in knowing that both your worth and your purpose are from the Lord and for the Lord. It is impossible to embrace these truths and not be changed by them.

Delight in who God says you are and who God calls you to be. For He alone is worthy! Let's live like it, shall we?

DAY 2:

Taking Steps to Walk Worthy

WHEN I LIVED WITH THE BELIEF that my worth was contingent on my performance, I walked the red-hot carpet of shame—a *lot*.

I was in a vicious cycle of striving to be perfect in everything I did so I would rank higher in the Father's eyes, only to fail and run from Him because I was entertaining the lie I was too far gone for Him to accept me. Eventually, I would turn back around and approach the Lord in the shame that weighed me down in order to beg Him for another chance.

I was constantly at war with myself and so very desperate for peace. For freedom.

The beautiful truth about belonging to the Lord is that our shame gets laid to rest. There is no room for it in our relationship with God. Conviction as a means of correction takes its place. Condemnation no longer exists for those who are in Christ. We get to draw near to the throne of grace not with shame but with the confidence that the Father is near and faithful to forgive all who call on His name!

The more we grow in our understanding of who God is and who we are because of what He has done for us, the more we will desire to live our lives full of reverence for Him.

Today we are going to look at some practical ways to intentionally and confidently walk in a manner worthy of the calling we have in Christ.

In Ephesians 4, we find a call for unity among God's people. Paul goes into detail, describing what it looks like to pursue a worthy walk. This passage offers practical steps for us to take so we will be mindful of the path we walk. Let's spend some time in this chapter.

Open your Bible to Ephesians 4:1-3 and list what it looks like to walk worthy in verse 2.

How do you think humility, gentleness, and patience help us walk worthy?

Which of these do you think you exhibit well? Which ones do you need to ask for God's help to grow in?

Humility

We are naturally prideful people. We may not like to admit it, but we are selfish to the core.

Our society only makes it worse with its ever-growing desire for instant gratification and enjoyment of pushing self-focused philosophies and ideologies.

In what ways do you struggle with pride?

That said, I do not think it is any coincidence that Paul lists humility as the first step to walking in a manner worthy (see Ephesians 4:2).

Christ shows us a *much* better way than we could ever pave for ourselves: a *humble* way. To pursue its path, we are to take on the mind of a servant.

Jesus offers us the most beautiful picture of humility.

Read Philippians 2:8. How did Jesus humble Himself?

Obedience to the point of death. This is the example we have in Christ.

Pursuing a life of humility might feel isolating at times, but we must remember we are not alone. We have all the recognition we need from the One who calls us by name, the One who is with us always (see Matthew 28:20).

To pursue the path of humility, seek first the Kingdom (seek the things of God over the things of this world), repent of your sins daily, read and obey what God commands us in His Word, think of others before yourself, be discerning about the words you speak, be willing to be mocked by the world, and *always* make it a point to give God thanks and praise.

As we do these things, our humility will increase. And as our humility increases, our pride will decrease.

What steps can you take this week to reject pride and grow in humility?

Gentleness

Turn in your Bible to Proverbs 15:1 (NLT) and write it in the space below.

Gentleness is rooted in the character of Christ. When we think of someone who is gentle, descriptors such as kind, loving, and respectful come to mind.

Who comes to mind when you think of gentleness? Why do you think of that person?

Take one look at the comments on a trending controversial social media post and the last thing you will find is gentleness. Harsh words and anger often reign. Gentleness is extremely underrated.

We live in a sad reality where people are quick to tear each other down and/or seek revenge rather than build each other up, extend forgiveness, and pursue reconciliation. The proof of our need for a Savior is everywhere we look.

Consider how Jesus treated those who hated Him. He knew very well how the scribes and Pharisees felt about Him, yet He loved them and pointed them to truth in the face of their hatred, all the way to the point of His death.

To pursue the path of gentleness, we must be a people who prioritize the call to be quick to hear and slow to speak (see James 1:19). We must make it a point to be a calm presence in the midst of conflict, speak the truth in love, be empathetic and mindful of the needs of others, and remember that we are an extension of Christ's love to everyone we come into contact with—including ourselves.

When we exhibit gentleness, we demonstrate our desire for the peace and harmony the Lord desires to see within the body of believers.

Where in your life might the Lord be calling you to gentleness?

Patience

Confession: patience is not my strong suit.

Waiting on something is not my cup of tea, and I appreciate instant gratification more than I would like to admit. If I want something, I am often tempted to find a way to get my hands on it as fast as possible.

Do you struggle with patience? If so, what does that look like?

As I am writing this, my husband, Michael, and I have been hoping, searching, and praying for a place to call home and raise our family for almost three years.

The wait has felt downright devastating at times, to both of us. Like a dream that is out of reach.

It has been really nice to walk through this together because we have been able to help each other keep our gaze on Christ and rest in the truth that God is faithful to provide our every need—dream home or not—and His will is nothing short of pleasing and perfect. That He has us *right* where He wants us, and we are surrounded by blessings upon blessings—dream home or not.

Going through the cycle of trusting and doubting the Lord has served as a powerful reminder to both Michael and me that our Father in heaven is more patient with us than we will ever be with Him. He cannot be rushed, and His perfect plans cannot be thwarted. He is faithful to be trusted at all times, in all ways.

We have so many different examples of patience in Scripture. Consider Abraham, who waited twenty-five years for God to fulfill His promise of a son. Or Joseph, who was sold into slavery by his brothers and endured years of trouble after trouble as a result—but ended up as Pharaoh's second-in-command, which gave him a beautiful opportunity to extend forgiveness to his brothers. Think about Mary, the mother of Jesus, who patiently and faithfully embraced the holy calling of a virgin birth, which would give us the Savior of the world.

As we seek to grow in our patience of trusting in God, let us not forget to acknowledge how patient our great God is with us. Whether we are waiting for God to answer a prayer, struggling to be patient with someone who is difficult, or struggling to be patient with ourselves, may we choose to rest without hesitation in the patience God offers us.

Are you catching the pattern for walking in a manner that is worthy of the calling we have received? It has everything to do with how we treat others.

Knowing this, take some time to sit with the following questions:

In what ways does my faith walk reflect my love for the Lord and demonstrate my love for His people?

What are some ways I can better love those around me?

DAY 3:
Walking toward Unity

I THOUGHT I DESPISED CHURCH GROWING UP. What I really did not like, however, was the church culture I was immersed in.

Even as a child, I could see through the facade. Perhaps you know it too. Wearing your Sunday best with your head held high, acting as if your life is perfect and only ever telling people you're doing great, even if you are suffering on the inside. I always felt like the odd duck out in this atmosphere because I knew that what I was experiencing was an inauthentic portrayal of God's design for the body.

I began to question the point of church if this was how it was going to be.

Thankfully, my desire to know God was not diminished by this experience. However, as I've mentioned before this point, it did result in an understanding of Him that was unbiblical in many ways. I had allowed my experience instead of God's Word to speak to my understanding of who He was because, simply put, I didn't know better. Although it felt like something was missing at the time, I was unable to get to the root of what that was until late high school when the Holy Spirit entered my hungry, searching heart.

The Power of the Local Church

Many Christians today will tell you church is not necessary, but I could not disagree more. Being part of a local church is beautiful, right, and biblical. It is first and foremost for God's glory but also for our good and the good of others. It is how we grow and learn to live in unity with one another. The church is not perfect, but it is God's vision for His people, so it is pleasing to Him.

A church that is built on the foundation of God's authoritative Word, deeply values sound doctrine, is in love with the glory of God, and is a place where you can come and be reminded of your sin and pointed to your need for Christ, is a church that reflects God's heart. This is the type of church where we belong.

What are some things you appreciate about your church?

How has the church impacted your walk with the Lord?

Yesterday we took a look at Ephesians 4:1-3, where Paul emphasizes the importance of walking in a manner worthy of the holy calling we have received in Christ Jesus. At the heart of the characteristics he shares—humility, gentleness, patience—is the call to unity. If we want to be a people of God who walk worthy, we must live in a way that demonstrates our desire for the unity God desires to see within the body of Christ.

Ephesians 4:4-6 tells us, "There is one body and one Spirit—just as you were called to the one hope that belongs to your call—one Lord, one faith, one baptism, one God and Father of all, who is over all and through all and in all."

What do believers share in Jesus (verses 5-6)?

How does baptism point to the unity of the church?

Maintaining Unity in the Church

We have unity because we share in the life of the One who has made a way to the Father. In Jesus, we share one body, one Spirit, one hope, one Lord, one faith, one baptism, and one God and Father of all. Because of our shared faith in Him, we get to share in the spiritual unity He offers.

As Christians, we already share in the unity offered to us by the Spirit, but we must work to maintain this unity within the church. How? By recognizing everyone has a role to play and equipping them to follow their callings.

Read Romans 12:3-8. How does this passage contribute to your understanding of your role within the church?

The church must value the call to faithfully steward the spiritual gifts God has imparted to its members. Pastors and teachers must concentrate on equipping the body, and members of the congregation must utilize the gifts God has given them to build up the body of Christ so that Christ is magnified (see Ephesians 4:11-13). The diligent efforts of the church and its dependency on the Lord to do this well is how the church is able to maintain unity.

What gifts has God given you? How might you use them for God's glory and the building up of the church?

In the New Testament, we find many "one another" commands for the church. Explore the following passages and make note of the "one another" commands found in each.

- Mark 9:50
- John 6:43
- Galatians 5:26
- Ephesians 4:32
- James 5:16

How do these commands equip us to walk in a manner worthy?

What would it look like for you to contribute to unity in your local church?

As we seek to maintain unity within the church, may the Lord grant us the ability not to focus on what divides us but on the One who brings us together despite our differences. May we be a people who walk in humility, gentleness, and patience, so the unity Christ made a way for would live and dwell within the church.

DAY 4:

Put on the New Self

IN CHRIST, WE ARE A NEW CREATION. This means we are no longer identified by the sins that once reigned over us. We are now daughters who have been purchased and set free by the atoning sacrifice of Christ, "because of his great love for us" (Ephesians 2:4, NIV). Our liberation in Christ means we become dead to our sins and alive in Him!

Turn to Ephesians 4:22-24. What are the three principles for Christian living Paul shares?

How does Paul describe the old self in Ephesians 2:1-3?

How does Paul describe the process of being made new in Ephesians 2:4-10?

This, my friend, is the Good News! Because of His rich mercy and grace, we have been redeemed and declared righteous. Hallelujah!

When we trust in Jesus as our Lord and Savior, the glorious gospel message changes us from the inside out through the power of the Holy Spirit at work in us. This is the beautiful reality of belonging to Christ: "He who began a good work in you will bring it to completion at the day of Jesus Christ" (Philippians 1:6). As we live in between Christ's resurrection and return, we will continue to be sanctified by our Father in heaven. God is at work in you right now, causing you to change, grow, and bear the beautiful image of Christ.

Putting on the New Self

How have you experienced the Spirit helping you to take off your "old self" and put on your "new self"?

We have a role to play in the act of putting on the new self too.

Turn to Colossians 3:1-17. List what Paul deems necessary for us to put on the new self.

Paul shares the lay of the land with us here.

As you keep these things in mind, be reminded of this: the very best way to prioritize God, make decisions that honor Him, and live with your mind set on the things that are holy, right, and good is to feed your heart, mind, and soul with God's Word.

The more we saturate our hearts in Scripture and pursue the things that are above, the more we will grow in our desire to repent and turn away from sin; the more we will long to be holy and imitate Christ; the more we will walk worthy in the unity the Lord calls us to.

As we put on the new self, we will begin to bear the fruit of the Spirit. The ways we interact with ourselves and those around us will also begin to change. We will start to be more mindful of exuding humility, gentleness, and patience.

Spend some time in prayer, asking the Lord to reveal any areas in which you might be pursuing sin instead of holiness.

It's important to remember that putting on the new self is not simply a choice we make once. It is a choice we must make over and over every single day until Christ's return. Although the old self no longer defines us, it still lurks and craves the attention we once gave it. The old self hates the new self and desperately desires to see us live a life infiltrated with darkness and sin instead of the freedom, light, and love of Christ.

How are you actively turning away from the old self and putting on the new self?

Until Christ's return, the war between the old and the new will continue within us. We *will* fail at putting on the new self as much as we should, but because of Christ in us, we have the assurance of God's mercy, grace, and forgiveness to cover and sustain us along the way. We have the promise of victory.

Following His Desires

Take a few minutes to list some things you can do next time you're tempted to fall back into the ways of your old self.

When you're tempted to follow the desires of your old self, run to the Father. Repent and ask Him for the strength to keep running into His arms, to have the strength to put the temptations of your flesh to death on a daily basis.

If you are questioning whether something you want to say or do is something you should actually see through, ask yourself the following questions: *Can I do this and call upon the name of Jesus? How does Scripture speak to this desire? Can I speak this desire and the name of Jesus in the same breath?*

May we live to become more like Christ in all we do. May we strive to put the desires of the flesh to death and choose to instead put on the robe of Christ's righteousness. May we daily be so overwhelmed by the Father's great love for us that we do not hesitate to run into His arms when we're faced with temptation.

We know who we belong to. Let us live in such a way that it puts this truth on full display. Let us rejoice and be glad in all that He has done, is doing, and will do.

DAY 5:
Walking toward Eternity

YOU MADE IT, MY FRIEND! The final day of this five-session study on the disciplines of delight has arrived. I pray you have been nothing short of blessed by the truths that have met you in these pages!

As we begin to wrap things up, I want to spend the rest of our time together filling our hearts with the most beautiful promise of all: the promise of eternity.

When you think about eternity, what comes to mind?

Your Work Matters

Did anything I did today actually matter?

Have you ever asked yourself this question? I sure have.

The things we do on this side of heaven can often feel unimportant and as if they do not hold much—if any—value. But the work of our hands matters, and it is important we embrace this truth rather than reject it—even if we cannot see what it is accomplishing in the moment.

Friend, do not discount the work you are doing right here, right now. Everything you do is purposed for the glory of God (see 1 Corinthians 10:31). Tangible evidence or not, "your labor is not in vain" (see 1 Corinthians 15:58).

What is your typical response when you get caught up in the mundane tasks of life?

When you find yourself struggling to believe purpose and value can be found where you stand, I encourage you to take it as a sign to shift your focus. By turning our gaze from an everyday perspective to an eternal one, we catch a glimpse of what is to come. When our focus is set on the Father's eternal glory, we find beauty in the mundane and exactly what we need for the season we are in. We are reminded that there are no meaningless moments when they are lived in service of our eternal, everlasting, almighty God.

When we're struggling with the meaning of our life and the devastation and grief that overwhelm this world, Ecclesiastes is a wise book to plant our hearts in.

Read Ecclesiastes 3:9-15. Describe how this passage makes you feel in the space below.

It can be difficult to believe this passage is filled with hope—that nothing we do in this life really matters—because many of Solomon's words here come across as hopeless. However, this is not the teacher's intent. Not all is doom and gloom! The teacher's point in sharing what he does is to remind us that what we have in God is not only enough, but that it matters more than anything else we experience in this world.

God uses the things we go through in this life to bring about His glory. Whether we are high on the mountaintop, low in the valley, or somewhere in between, God is working to impart wisdom to our hearts, propel us forward in faith, remind us that He alone is our stability, and enable us to make Christ known.

Ecclesiastes reminds us that God sees all things, knows all things, and uses all things—the love and hate, scattering and gathering, tearing and mending, weeping and laughter (see verses 3:1-8). *Everything.*

Made for Eternity

As we put in the effort to keep our eyes on Him, we will come to recognize the eternal value of this life and have reason to rejoice for all that is to come.

Open your Bible to Ecclesiastes 3:11. What has God put in our hearts?

In what ways do you long for eternity?

As we await Christ's final return, I urge you to live out the truth that is embedded in your soul: the truth that we were made for more than the temporary things of this world.

My sister, I urge you to make it your life's goal to magnify Christ in *all* you do. The season you find yourself in right now is not a coincidence. God is not a God of happenstance. What He says will be, will be. As you seek to make more of Him, using the lens of eternity to view where your feet are planted is sure to infuse meaning into your life.

A great way to keep your eyes lifted up is to live out the disciplines of delight.

List the five disciplines of delight we have studied together in the space below.

1.

2.

3.

4.

5.

Which discipline are you most excited about? Which discipline do you think will be the most challenging for you? Why?

As we participate in these disciplines, let us also incorporate acts throughout our day that speak to the promise of eternity! Start each day anew in God's Word, fill the walls of your home with worship music, listen to podcasts that point you to Christ, serve your church body in the ways God has gifted you, join a small group (or lead one!), and pray and give thanks for the breath that continues to fill your lungs. Pour out your praise and thanks to God in the way you live your life.

Take some time to reflect on what your average day looks like in this season. As you do so, prayerfully consider ways in which you can bring more of Christ into your daily life.

When our focus is not on just getting through the present moment but rather on infusing the present with God's eternal glory, we are sure to find beauty in the mundane and grace for the season at hand.

You have an important role in expanding the Kingdom of God. When you find yourself weary and wondering, refuse to buy into the lie that why you are here and what you are doing is meaningless. That could not be any further from the truth. Instead, regardless of whether you see fruit from your work in this life, take heart in knowing that your efforts will certainly be worthwhile when you stand before the Lord and hear the words, "Well done, good and faithful servant" (Matthew 25:21).

Everything we do has meaning. May you never forget this.

For one day, we will spend all our days in eternity with the One who planted eternity in our hearts. Praise God!

May our eternal God give us the eyes to see and behold the beauty and purpose that He has woven into our lives. May we plant our hearts in the truth that His plan for us is wrapped in the promise of eternity. May we pursue sound doctrine, imitate Christ, hate what is evil, spread the gospel, and walk in a manner worthy. May we rejoice that eternity is surely on its way and be bold extensions of Christ's truth, light, and love as we await His glorious return. May we live as His daughters of delight.

Notes

SESSION 1: PURSUE SOUND DOCTRINE

Day 1: It Starts with Us

1. A. W. Tozer, *The Knowledge of the Holy: The Attributes of God. Their Meaning in the Christian Life* (Cambridge, UK: Lutterworth Press, 2022), 1.

Day 2: How Not to Read Your Bible

1. David Guzik, "John 5—A Healing and a Discourse," Enduring Word, 2018, https://enduringword.com/bible-commentary/john-5/.

Day 3: Questioning Scripture

1. David Guzik, "1 Corinthians 13—Agape Love," Enduring Word, 2018, https://enduringword.com/bible-commentary/1-corinthians-13/.

Day 4: Analyzing and Applying Scripture

1. "The Gospel of Matthew: Authorship," Blue Letter Bible, accessed March 15, 2024, https://www.blueletterbible.org/study/intros/matthew.cfm.
2. "The Gospel of Matthew: Authorship," Blue Letter Bible.
3. "Matthew: Introduction to Matthew," Blue Letter Bible, accessed March 15, 2024, https://www.blueletterbible.org/study/eo/Mat/Mat000.cfm.
4. "The Gospel of Matthew: Authorship," Blue Letter Bible.

SESSION 2: IMITATE CHRIST

Day 1: The Goal of Every Christian: Imitating Christ

1. "Chuck Smith: Verse by Verse Study on John 13–14," Blue Letter Bible, accessed March 15, 2024, https://www.blueletterbible.org/Comm/smith_chuck/c2000_Jhn/Jhn_013.cfm?a=1010005.
2. "John 8," Barclay's Daily Study Bible, StudyLight.org, accessed March 15, 2024, https://www.studylight.org/commentaries/eng/dsb/john-8.html.

Day 3: The Fruit of Imitation

1. Dietrich Bonhoeffer, *Life Together: The Classic Exploration of Christian Community* (New York: HarperCollins, 1954), 20.

Day 4: Remember in Order to Remain

1. "1 Thessalonians 2:14-16 Commentary," Precept Austin, updated May 3, 2023, https://www.preceptaustin.org/1thessalonians_214-16.

SESSION 3: HATE WHAT IS EVIL

Beware of Fool's Gold

1. "What Is 'Fool's Gold'?," U.S. Geological Survey, accessed March 15, 2024, https://www.usgs.gov/faqs/what-fools-gold.
2. Kathy Feick, "Pyrite," University of Waterloo, accessed March 15, 2024, https://uwaterloo.ca/earth-sciences-museum/resources/detailed-rocks-and-minerals-articles/pyrite.

SESSION 4: SPREAD THE GOSPEL

Day 1: Boldness Embodied

1. "David Guzik: Study Guide for Matthew 12," Blue Letter Bible, accessed March 15, 2024, https://www.blueletterbible.org/comm/guzik_david/study-guide/matthew/matthew-12.cfm?a=950012.

Day 5: Faithful Living in a Faithless World

1. "Jamieson, Fausset & Brown: Commentary on Daniel 1," Blue Letter Bible, accessed March 15, 2024, https://www.blueletterbible.org/Comm/jfb/Dan/Dan_001.cfm?a=851002.

About the Author

ELLE CARDEL is first and foremost a sinner saved by grace. She lives in middle Tennessee with her college sweetheart, Michael, and their two lovely children, Selah and Aidan. Elle loves being a mama, nerding out over strategy board games with Michael, catching up over coffee with friends (all the lavender lattes, please!), making meals from scratch, and writing on the truths of the glorious gospel of our Lord Jesus Christ.

Elle holds a bachelor's degree in biblical theology and is the founder of the global online women's ministry Daughter of Delight, a growing community of 175,000 plus women of faith. Elle is a firm believer that, in order to truly know God, we must know His Word. She is deeply passionate about equipping everyday women of faith with the tools to be faithful stewards of Bible literacy. She lives on a mission to help others learn and love Scripture via the *Daughter of Delight* podcast, daily devotionals woven around the Word, and free biblical resources. You can connect with Elle on Instagram, Facebook, and her website, daughterofdelight.com.

DAUGHTEROFDELIGHT.COM

@SHEDELIGHTS

@DAUGHTEROFDELIGHT

JOIN ELLE CARDEL
AS SHE HELPS US DEVELOP A HEART OF DELIGHT FOR GOD AND HIS WORD!

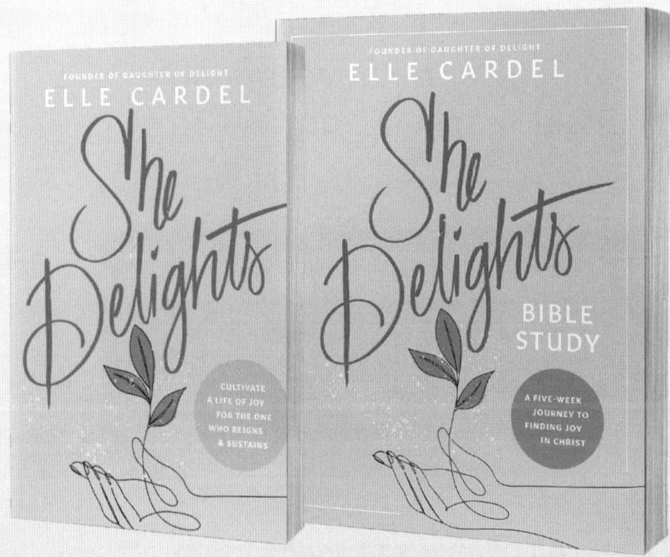

In *She Delights*, Elle Cardel seeks to challenge and encourage women of faith to be steadfast in our pursuit of and delight in God in every moment. She explores characteristics of God alongside different seasons of the Christian life and shows us how we can truly delight in Him through it all.

In the accompanying Bible study, joy is the hallmark of your next five weeks. Perfect for group or personal use, this study practically equips readers to see what an honor it is to delight in God's ways over our own and encourages us to continuously seek the delight of God in all things.

AVAILABLE WHEREVER BOOKS ARE SOLD.

CP2006